Don McCullough

DANNY BOY

A Memoir

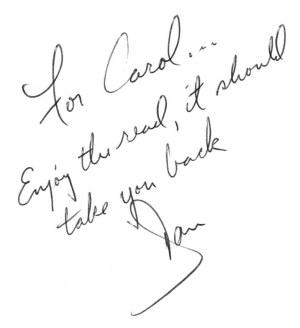

For Carol...
Enjoy the read, it should
take you back

Don

outskirtspress
DENVER, COLORADO

Outskirts Press, Inc.
http://www.outskirtspress.com

ISBN: 978-1-4787-2043-0

Outskirts Press and the "OP" logo are trademarks belonging to Outskirts Press, Inc.

PRINTED IN THE UNITED STATES OF AMERICA

For Kristin,
you saw through me
then saw me through

TABLE OF CONTENTS

Prologue vii

The Paradise 1

Paradise Lost 65

A Brave New World 97

When Worlds Collide 118

The Wanting Disciple 142

The Year of Trepidation 154

Away 170

Epilogue 176

Credits & Acknowledgements 192

Even in our sleep pain which cannot be borne falls drop by drop upon our heart until, against our will and by the awful grace of God, becomes wisdom.

Aeschylus

PROLOGUE

August 1999

"...But come ye back when summer's in the meadow..."

I squatted on my haunches in the carefully landscaped grass. My left knee cracked, making me wince. My hands, rough and calloused from years of hard service, dangled between my knees. I gazed over the ground, squinting in the unrelenting sun. It had been many years since I'd been here in this place, since I was a teenager. I was now in my forties. The land, like me, had changed much. Where I now crouched had once been bucolic pastureland dotted with groves of pecan, oak, and mesquite trees. In my youth, Hereford cattle grazed, and cattle paths had crisscrossed the pastures, marking the way from watering tank to watering tank to feed stations. Gone were the beloved forests of my youth.

My boyhood home and surrounding land had once been at the very edge of this north Texas grain mill town. All that open land, broken here and there with dark and wild woodland and winding creek beds where once I hunted for prehistoric shark teeth with my friends, were long gone. I found myself in the midst a well-manicured, upper-middle-class suburban enclave. "McMansions," I mused. I smiled, creasing the lines of my face as I wondered who might be peeking out of their windows at the stranger crouching in the hot, midday sun.

I looked down at the cut grass under my feet. Bluebonnets grew here in the long grasses of the pastures I knew in another lifetime. Grasshoppers hid, camouflaged in green and brown, ready to flee in hordes as you walked through. I had stood here on this gentle rise a long time ago. I was certain. I had stood here, feeling the earth weep. I could feel her now beneath my feet, under the trim, alien grass.

I looked out over the large man-made pond that I had spent so many summers swimming and fishing in. At least it was still here, I thought. Otherwise, I would've been disoriented as to where I was, what with all the changes. The home of my childhood lay just on the other side and below the earthen dam that contained it. The backyard of my home backed up to the bottom of the dam, which then rose about twenty feet up a steep bank to the water on the other side. Tanks, they were called, formed by ranchers damming up a spring or creek to create watering holes for their cattle.

Looking beyond the pond and dam I scanned the horizon. My old neighborhood fell away in a gentle slope into the treetops. In the view beyond lay expansive pastures, new residential developments, and treetops lining meandering creeks. My gaze lingered, looking northward toward the big lake they called Texoma. I stood still as a memory, surprising in its clarity, came to my mind of the night up there during summer camp that forever changed me.

⸺◆⸺

I remembered stumbling blindly out of the tent. The candy, the fun, and the laughter were forgotten in the darkness. My body ached with pain from all the punches I'd absorbed. I was barely aware of Billy stumbling alongside me in the pitch-black beneath the trees. Both of us had left our flashlights behind.

Fresh tears erupted. A snot bubble burst from my nostril. I spat several times and tried but couldn't think clearly. All I could remember was Stevie looming menacingly over me, the laughter from the other boys, and Stevie's dangerous voice. I tried to block everything from my mind, especially Stevie, but couldn't. Everything was a blur while at the same time things stood out in crystal clarity.

"Everyone was laughin' at me," I croaked. I glanced toward Billy, unable to look him in the eye. "Did you laugh too?"

"No," was all Billy Swift said.

We made it back to our tent and undressed wordlessly in the dark. I felt ruined. I curled up in a tight ball in my sleeping bag, crying to myself as I waited desperately for sleep. It was a long time coming.

⇒—

"You were just a boy," I whispered to myself as I looked northward toward a night from long ago. I rose to my feet, my knee cracking again. I looked around at the scant signs and remnants of the land of my youth. An old ache moaned faintly in the farthest reaches of my heart, like a distant train whistle, ancient by the time it is heard. A door swung open in my mind as more memories of my boyhood here poured out like children spilling out through the doors on the last day of school.

THE PARADISE

"Oh Danny boy, the pipes, the pipes are calling
From glen to glen, and down the mountain side..."

I crouched in the tall, dry grass of the ravine, listening. Just in front of me stood an earthen mound about four feet high, an odd remnant from one of the spring floods that rioted down the ravine from the tank every year. The sun poured through the canopy of oak and pecan trees, dappling the ground below.

"Do you see them yet?" I whispered.

My friend Billy Swift crept up the mound and peeked over the grassy top. He called back over his shoulder. "They're comin' up the creek now!"

I crept up alongside my friend. Billy wore round, wire-rimmed glasses and had BO as usual. I didn't care. Billy Swift was a fun guy and my best friend. We spent hours together in his bedroom, building car models and reading our favorite magazines like *Mad* and *Road & Track*. We discussed in earnest the kind of cars we would have when we turned sixteen. At age twelve, Billy was already an accomplished drummer, and we would take turns at his five-piece Pearl drum set with Billy trying patiently, but vainly, to teach me some rudiments.

"Man, they don't even know we're here," I whispered gleefully. Peeking over the top, I saw Paul and Chris farther down the ravine, creeping in our direction. They were looking around in every direction except ours. My excitement grew. Our ambush was going to work perfectly. I had a sudden urge to pee.

Billy raised a hand in front of me. "Shhh. Wait…. wait."

Paul and Chris moved ever closer along the ravine floor, heads turning side to side. Overhead in the trees cicadas buzzed in their incessant rising and falling call. Mockingbirds sang and scissortails swooped through the hot, still air.

"Wait…. wait…. almost…. NOW!"

Billy and I sprang up and opened fire with our Mattel machine guns and rained an imaginary hail of bullets down on Paul and Chris, who stood rooted to the spot in realization that those two little shits up there on the mound had actually gotten them.

"You're dead!" we screamed. "*Blattablattablatta!* You're dead! You're dead! We got ya! Hahahaha!"

In keeping with the rigid code of playing war, Paul and Chris glumly went through the motions of dying, clutching their abdomens and grimacing up at the sky.

"Ahhh," they both intoned. "Ya got me. Ya got me."

Looking before they actually went down to the ground in case they landed on a tarantula, or worse yet, a mound of fire ants, Paul and Chris slowly crumbled to the ground.

"Ya hafta stay like that for one minute!" I hollered. "Start countin'!"

Paul and Chris began counting in monotone. "One, two, three, four…."

"Slower!" yelled Billy Swift.

"This is slow!" Paul yelled back. "Ya better get goin'!"

Billy and I scrambled down the mound and lit off up the ravine toward the large culvert pipe that ran under the street and into the woods beyond, laughing and whooping as we ran.

"We got those Krauts!" Billy cried. "Got 'em good! Those Nazis never had a chance."

"Yeah!" I said. "'Cause we're the U.S. Army, and we won the war! The Germans never had a chance!"

We tore through the culvert pipe into the woods. Taking cover, we crouched under a tangled thicket of dried grapevine hanging from an ancient pecan tree. Billy Swift snapped off a couple of dried twigs about the length of a cigarette and handed one to me. He pulled a crumpled book of matches out of his shorts pocket, put the grapevine twig to his mouth and lit it, drawing a big puff. He extended the lit match in his cupped hands to me, who was ready with my grapevine cigarette. Together we sat and smoked, enjoying the dry, sweet taste.

"Remember," Billy said, "you only light two off one match, never three. Snipers always get the third guy. My dad said so. They used to do that in the war."

"My dad never talks about the war," I said.

Suddenly we heard the voice of my mother calling my name. "Oh, man," I groaned. "Wait! Oh yeah. *Daktari*'s coming on! I gotta go watch it."

"I hate *Daktari*," Billy Swift said. "Who cares about Africa anyway?"

"It's cool! Last week a lion killed one of the natives and they blamed it on Clarence!"

"I know. I saw that one."

"Ha! So you watch it too!"

My mother's voice again, calling louder in the late-afternoon air.

"Coming!" I yelled back at the top of my voice. Billy and I snubbed out our grapevine cigarettes and emerged from the thicket.

"There they are!"

Billy and I spun around to see Paul and Chris running from out of the culvert pipe, toy guns blazing.

"Gotcha! Gotcha!" the risen enemy Nazis exclaimed triumphantly.

"No fair, dickweed," Billy Swift shot back. He pointed at me. "His mother gave us away, and he's gotta go in."

"So what?" Paul yelled back. "Gotcha anyway!"

"Buttholes!" I yelled. "I'm gonna go watch *Daktari,* then I hafta eat. Game's over. I quit."

"We didn't get a chance to ambush you, and we even let you be the good guys this time," Chris complained.

"You get to be the good guys next time," Billy Swift said, shrugging.

"Next time we play war at the old dairy," Chris said. "You guys are gonna be the bad guys!"

"See ya later," I said to them and turned for home.

I scrambled up the embankment to the street and began running. With knobby knees covered with scabs protruding below cut-off jean shorts pumping in unison with my hands that I held just like my hero Bullet Bob Hayes did, I ran barefoot on the blazing asphalt until I could no longer stand the heat burning my feet. I slowed, moving to the side of the road where the concrete gutter lining the street was much cooler. The bottoms of my feet, like all the other kids', were tough as leather. More than once my mother, a nurse at the town's white hospital, broke pin needles while attempting to lance the occasional blood blister the heated asphalt caused.

Sixth grade had ended the week before, and it was now my favorite time of year; summer vacation. It stretched out gloriously before me. It was the beginning of June 1968. I was twelve years old. It was the beginning of the end for me.

═══◆═══

My family was a large, warm, loud and boisterous Irish-Catholic clan of six children. Two girls, Colleen and Eileen, were followed in quick succession by four boys, me, Timmy, Willie, and Bobby. Mother and Father, products of the Great Depression, were frugal, practical, and typical.

Dad's work was a bit of a boring mystery to me. I observed that he got up every morning, put on a white shirt and tie, and left in a company car for the "plant." What went on at the "plant" was unknown to me, and I wasn't much concerned. My dad had fought in the war and been a football hero, which was pretty much all I cared about.

Mother was a matriarch of the first degree. Fiercely protective of family, hearth, and home, she was a loyalist of the highest order to the church, being Irish and being American. She had finished college with a degree in nursing from a fine school in New York City then dutifully, predictably, set aside any plans and married our father and started a family.

After thirteen years producing six children, she picked up an anatomy and physiology textbook, which my brothers and I privately thrilled over, gazing at the illustrations of breasts, laughing at the penises, and puzzling over the mysterious reproductive organs of the female of the species. After studying the book for a few months, privately wondering where the all dirty smudge marks came from, she took the state board examination and obtained her nursing license. When the youngest of the brood hit the first grade, off she went to work at one of the two hospitals in town. She chose the semiprivate hospital on the west side of town over the community hospital across town in the Negro section. It was closer to home she said.

This set up a summer living situation in which Eileen was designated as the summertime babysitter for us boys, as Colleen was already working a steady summer job. Although only fifteen when she started babysitting the previous summer, Eileen was the right choice for the job. She could be a tyrant. A tomboy and gifted athlete, she had a booming voice and great right hook that she wasn't afraid to use. Now sixteen and with a year of watching her brothers under her belt, she had us broken in and in tow.

She recently started smoking cigarettes and inviting neighborhood boys over to the house, summarily exiling us boys to the great outdoors, leaving us to our own devices and sworn to secrecy about her doings from Mother. But she did have a driver's license now, which meant we could now easily reach the municipal pool. Many were the days when Eileen would simply pull up, drop us off, and drive off with the boyfriend of the day. So long as no bones were broken or no one was missing at dinnertime and the police weren't summoned, all was good. The rules were simple. Be home for dinner, and after dinner be home again when the streetlights came on.

⋯⬥⋯

Summer vacation bloomed before me, and within a week I had shrugged off the last vestiges of school-year routine and settled into the lazy, slow life of a twelve year old well adapted to the scrutiny of a wide-open Texan sky and its withering sun. *Dialing For Dollars* was a morning staple. My brothers and I could never understand why the telephone book the show's host used to randomly dial a number to ask the unwitting twerp on the other end what the dollar amount he was giving away never began with our hometown exchange. We wondered why didn't those stupid people on the other end of the phone just turn on the TV and look at the dollar amount plainly displayed on the host's podium, instead of sleepily asking again who was it they were speaking to and then, exasperated, take a wild guess at a number. They were never right. What's wrong with people? I vowed daily to always know the dollar amount each and every morning. A couple hundred bucks would ensure the success of the biggest secret I kept from my family.

Tired of having to share everything with my brothers all the time, which included our bedroom, feeling burdened with an unfair measure of household chores and living under the thumb of a bossy older sister, I had secretly decided to run away and strike out for my freedom. I felt it was high time I should be living on my own.

Tucked into the back of my designated shelf of the chiffarobe in the bedroom, under my underwear where I knew grubby hands would not venture, I kept a Rand McNally atlas of the United States. Each night I would sneak off from the family, no small feat in a house with eight people, take the atlas out, and open the tattered book to the page that displayed the state of Texas. Texas was so big it needed two pages. I liked that. I lived in the best state there is 'cause it took two whole pages to display it. And each and every night I would plot my escape from my family in our town not far from the Red River, town by town, until I had walked clear to Mexico.

By my calculation, it would take about a week, provided I walked every day and made each town along the way on schedule. Looked easy enough to me on the map. Besides, people in Texas were friendly and would give me a drink of water whenever I asked for it. The really friendly people, ranchers mostly, would offer Dr. Pepper.

From my home I'd take Highway 82 west to the next town, Whitesboro. Highway 82 was just a few hundred yards from my back door, past the tank that was beyond my backyard. At night I could hear the sound of eighteen-wheelers working up through the gears as they left town and into the open rolling land, their humming tires on the road lulling me to sleep. In the town after that, Greenville, I'd probably get something to eat. I'd keep walking, all the way to Wichita Falls. From there, the route turned southwest toward Abilene.

The route was painstakingly plotted each night. No leg of the journey was too far. There were plenty of towns along the route till I reached my final destination: Cuidad Juarez. I'd been there once during one of our ritual family summer vacations. I'd bought the sombrero I had tacked up on my bedroom wall there. I would join the other kids I'd seen there, standing ankle deep in the measly, muddy Rio Grande. I had watched them holding long sticks up in the air affixed with cones they fashioned out of cardboard at the tips that they used to catch pennies the tourists threw over the railing of the pedestrian bridge at them. It seemed grand! I would make enough each day to eat sno-cones and have french fries at a local Dairy Queen there. I was sure they had a Dairy Queen in Cuidad Juarez.

⟱

Before I bolted to Mexico, however, there was plenty of fun to be had in the neighborhood. It was geographically separated from the rest of the town, being a recent suburban development carved out of a slice of ranch land on the western edge of the city limits. The only road leading into it came off Highway 82 as it wound westward out of town. It was our very own kingdom, safe from any foreign invasion of children from other neighborhoods.

Altogether there were a dozen or so boys who fell in with each other, ranging from fifth graders up to ninth graders, making for lively games of football, the reigning religion of Texas. Boys younger than that were ignored. Boys older than that ignored us. Girls were regarded warily. Some were tough enough to play and thus respected. Some were, well, pretty and thus to be feared by the mystery surrounding the private thoughts and fantasies of all us boys.

We played across the yards of the neighborhood, with the prize lawns being the ones lacking the insidious pea-sized barbed seeds of the tough, wide blade grass used to sod the yards throughout Texas. When we tired of football, we rode shiny Schwinn Stingray bikes with banana seats and sissy bars pell-mell through the streets and the one narrow alley that ran between the two parallel rows of houses in the lower part of the neighborhood, providing plenty of high-speed close calls and other scary moments. Once, Robbie Mobley sailed his bike over a jump and through a screened backyard patio, shattering a glass coffee table.

We stationed homemade jumps made from two-by-fours and scrap plywood at various points. The highest jumps were applauded, and the weak ones jeered. Billy Swift was a pro at popping wheelies and riding down the road on his rear wheel. I tried hard to emulate him. A favorite game was Follow-the-Leader on our bikes through the woods and pastures, riding at breakneck speeds along the cow paths, daring each other to keep up as we flew at the very edge of our riding skills.

By far, the most extravagant and exciting endeavor undertaken by all the boys that summer was the building and racing of homemade go-carts. The topography of the neighborhood was tailor-made for hosting a string of racing tournaments throughout the long summer. Starting with the road that ran in front of the tank on which my home was situated, the neighborhood sloped gently downward and away. A long, U-shaped street began in front of my home that led down through the neighborhood, curved to the left and out of sight from my house and then left again, rising till it met my road again four houses up from mine. The long gentle slope of the road with its straightaway made for a perfect Soapbox Derby track.

Made of rough scrap wood nailed together and equipped with metal roller skate wheels liberated from their uppers, a length of rope was tied to each outside end of the front crosspiece to steer with. We careened down the street yanking the rope left or right, depending upon the frequent obstacle confronting the driver as they sped downhill. Usually the obstacle was a preceding driver who had experienced a structural failure of some sort and was stranded in the middle of the road. Racing side by side was perilous. Collisions were frequent.

So frequent were the accidents that I had the idea to attach a cardboard box to my go-cart in which I carried a bottle of peroxide and cotton balls pilfered from my mother's medicine cabinet. I used it liberally on the numerous cases of road rash experienced by the racers after accidents. Positioning my go-cart off to the side of the starting line, I would sit and watch as the others raced two by two down the street. I wouldn't have to wait long before pointing my cart downhill, heading to the scene of another wreck where I would grind myself to a halt with the heels of my PF Fliers and jump off with the peroxide and cotton balls to administer to a grimacing kid, making him dance and wince when I applied the foaming, bubbling solution. All the kids appreciated my efforts, so I painted the word "ambulance" on the side of my go-cart.

However, a far greater disaster awaited all of us.

At the height of ambition, seeking the ultimate thrill, Rusty Howard one day produced a twelve-foot long plank of wood ten inches wide and two inches thick.

Pushing his black-framed glasses up on his nose, he stretched his arms out and tilted his face theatrically up in the air. The others around looked at him curiously. He cleared his throat and made his pronouncement.

"We're gonna build a go-cart made for ten!" he grandly exclaimed to the gathered bunch.

Rusty Howard was real smart, and an Eagle Scout as well. If he said it could be done, no one doubted it. Roller wheels were cannibalized from other go-carts, usually from ones destroyed in previous crashes. Hammers and nails borrowed from fathers' workbenches and all the wood necessary for construction, including the twelve foot plank, were hauled to the top of the long street, where the road abruptly ended in front of a long barbed wire fence marking the end of civilization and the start of ranch land.

Under Rusty's supervision, the ten-man go-cart took shape. Rusty even engineered the placement of a set of roller skate wheels midship under the long carrying plank. A thick, six inch long bolt with extra washers was used to ensure maneuverability for the front crosspiece. The metal wheels resisted easy steering, being designed essentially to travel in straight lines. At last, the project was finished. Everyone stood back to admire it. We looked to Rusty for further leadership.

"Okay," he said, "here's the lineup beginning with me. I do the steering."

A clamor erupted on the remaining order of bodies. "Me! No, me! Me next! Pick me! Pick me!"

Rusty consulted with the next older boy, Stevie Walsh, who was going into the tenth grade. They agreed Stevie would be last on the rig to balance out the weight and the others were divvied up from there.

I was randomly selected to be second behind Rusty. I was thrilled. I had been on camping trips with Rusty and the Scout troop we all belonged to for the past two years and always felt safe with Rusty in the bunch. Rusty knew cool ways to start campfires without using matches, knew all his knots, and knew first aid as well. He taught me how to manually open a can of Dinty Moore stew and cook it on a rock ringing the fire without burning myself or getting a bunch of ash in the can. I thought being named second on the go-cart behind Rusty was a high honor.

When the order was complete, the behemoth go-cart, nicknamed "Shitty-shitty-bang-bang," was moved into position with a rock placed under one of the front wheels, keeping it in place as we got on one by one. A few mothers appeared at their front doors looking up the street with a mixture of bemusement and concern. They all trusted Rusty. He was a very responsible kid. But my, that was one big go-cart.

At the top of the hill Rusty glanced back over his shoulder after everyone got on. "Stevie," he called, "everyone all set?"

Stevie glanced down the line. Sneering, he called out. " Any of you pussies wanna chicken out?" Stevie was a bit feared by the young-er boys. He was a gifted athlete, ensuring his high rank among us, but could be a cruel bully too. We excitedly adjusted ourselves on the long plank, grasping the tee shirt of the one in front of us and hooking our legs around their waist. Excitement reigned. No one got off.

"Let 'er go!" Stevie called out.

With that, Rusty reached out a foot and kicked loose the rock holding back the go-cart. At first, nothing happened; such was the weight of this never-before-seen marvel and the ten boys crammed on to it. Rusty gave a few quick body movements forward to coax the rig onward.

"C'mon, guys," Rusty called over his shoulder, "help out a little, will ya?"

Everyone joined in, jerking ourselves forward several times to get "Shitty-shitty-bang-bang" off to a start. The silliness of it made us all laugh. Slowly, the large vehicle started forward. Metal roller wheels grinded on the pavement. Rusty gave a few more forward body jerks to build speed. The go-cart began gathering momentum, and Rusty held her steady straight down the middle of the street. Peals of excited laughter rang out.

"Hold on to your peckers, everyone!" Stevie jeered loudly over the sound of the wheels.

I craned my neck to look over the shoulder of the older, taller Rusty. A hot breeze blew over me. I squeezed my legs tighter around Rusty's waist. Adrenalin bloomed in my belly. "Shitty-shitty-bang-bang" began to gather steam.

The noise of the metal wheels on pavement grew louder, mixing with whoops and cries for more speed. Rusty gamely kept the whole thing straight on course, but steering began to get harder.

There was no jumping off now without risk to body and limb. Peals of laughter began to give way to more serious exclamations. Only Stevie remained undeterred, regaling all those aboard and the gathered spectators with colorful and profane warnings against being a chicken.

With gaining speed, the go-cart careened down the street. Rusty fought to keep her on course. Long hair flew in the wind. Sweat dried on the skin. The noise of the wheels grew louder.

Days later, someone would say it was the revenge of all the toads ever run over flat in the street. During the long hot summers big fat toads hopping across the roads of Texas became daily road kill. So ubiquitous were they that the ones dried most by the pavement and unrelenting sun were used by the boys to throw like skipping stones at each other, younger kids, and squealing girls.

As Rusty tried to steer to avoid it, he watched in growing dismay as a fat toad began hopping across the street as the go-cart bore down on it.

"Rusty!" I shouted, looking over his shoulder. "Rusty! Look out!"

Too late. The left front wheel ran smack into the toad. The big rig jerked to the left. To ensure that fate would seal the disaster, the same left front wheel then hit an already flattened and dried toad. The combination of fresh kill mixed with old kill was enough to gum up the wheel and make Rusty lose control of the steering. The go-cart continued its leftward veer, and we watched in horror at the fast-approaching concrete curb. Rusty fought valiantly to steer toward a driveway and up into a yard, but he no longer had control. Each of us knew this was going to end badly. Our speed was too great. There was no choice but to hang on to each other and hope for the best.

"AAAAAAUUUUUUGGGGGGGHHHHH!" was the collective wail that rose as the huge go-cart crunched into the curb. The front cross piece, so well bolted to the main plank, snapped off, splinter-ing in all directions. The main carrying plank lurched to the right and nose-dived into the asphalt, launching horrified victims into the air in a tangled mass of body and limb. Bodies landed in a moving heap in the road. Wails and cries went up, and mothers bolted from their doors toward the catastrophe.

As we crashed back to earth, my foot somehow become lodged between the pavement and Rusty's rear end, scraping it raw as mo-mentum continued to hurl all of us down the street. Billy Swift came crashing down on top of me, knocking the wind out of me.

Finally, everything came to rest. Although at first everyone was too dazed to move, the heat of the asphalt in the midday sun drove us blindly off the street and into a yard where we collapsed wailing. Adding to our misery, the yard was full of those nasty pricker seeds.

Our cries grew louder. Like Icarus flying too close to the sun, the grandest scheme yet devised in the neighborhood had crashed spectacularly back to earth. It took the rest of the summer for the road rash to heal. I came to wear the scar on my foot trapped under Rusty's skinny rear end with pride.

Throughout the rest of the summer we would point to our healing scars and say to each other, "See that? That was from the 'Shitty-shitty-bang-bang' ride." It always drew ooohs and ahhs as each of us would take turns displaying our various wounds and giving each other the proper mutual respect.

⟫

I ran through the garage and threw open the door that led through the utility room into the family den.

"Ma! Maaa!" I cried, running through the house. "Ma! Maaaaa!"

"Jeez Louise!" exclaimed my mother from the upstairs master bedroom. A pile of clean laundry lay on the bed. A cigarette dangled from the corner of her mouth. "No need to be so loud!" she yelled.

I bounded up the stairs. "Can I go campin'?" I said breathlessly. "Can I? Everyone's goin'! Huh? Can I?"

"No." Reflexive. Automatic. Protective.

"Maaaaaa!" I wailed. "Why not? C'mon, Ma! Can I? Please? Please?"

"A bunch of boys don't need to be out in the woods unsupervised. What if an accident happened?"

"It's just to the Swiss Family Robinson tree. Nothin's gonna happen. Everybody's got a flashlight. It's still daylight."

She wavered. A maternal fear of having any of her brood out of sight and sound under less-than-ideal circumstances was strong. Fear had always been a motivator and rationale to limit her children's curiosity of the world around them, and it usually worked. The neighbor's trampoline was off-limits because it would end up causing paralysis.

The area under the train trestle was out of bounds because bums lived underneath it. The "devil's path," a name given by the kids to a long narrow path that twisted along one of the creeks was out of bounds because "bad men" stayed there. Never mind that it was in the middle of a pasture, a mere fifty yards from the neighborhood. I often wondered just who all the bums and bad men were. I'd never seen any. Playing with one's own penis would result in its removal by God. I still had mine, and as far as I could tell no boy I knew was without one. The Good Humor Man's ice cream was no good because it gave you diarrhea. I never knew any of my friends to suffer that affliction. But my mother had been adamant. My growing independence, however, was a new reckoning.

"There's not enough daylight left," she said with diminishing conviction.

"All I need is my sleepin' bag an' flashlight! We're only going over near the creek behind the Parker's house. You know, where the Swiss Family Robinson tree is! There's plenty of time! Please? C'mon, please?"

Exasperated, my mother stopped folding the shirt in her hands and looked upward. "Go ahead, I don't care," she conceded. "Take some PJs and clean underwear."

"Ma!" I cried. "I'll be home in the mornin'! I don't need that stuff!"

"Well, brush your teeth anyway before you go."

"Aww, c'mon! No one else is. Can't I just go? Please?"

"Go ahead!" she cried in final surrender to my onslaught.

"Can I take the rest of the Cheese Doodles?"

She growled and looked down at me. The laundry still needed folding. She fixed me with a glare.

I knew that look. I'd reached the limit. But I was cleared for departure. I whooped and bolted out of the room. In the end, as I was leaving the house, I grabbed the half-eaten bag of Cheese Doodles, quickly stuffed it into the middle of my threadbare sleeping bag and slipped out through the garage before any of my brothers spotted me and wanted to come along.

There were nine of us that gathered under the majesty of the Swiss Family Robinson tree. None of us knew what kind of tree she was. We only knew she was the best tree in all the woods. She was magical. It was perfectly situated in the middle of a large sandbar that jutted into a muddy, slow-moving creek. She was ancient and aptly named by the children. It was so high no one had yet been brave enough to climb to the top. It took five boys to ring the base of her trunk. Huge, thick branches grew low from her, sweeping gracefully out in all directions, almost touching the ground in some places. There was no need really to summit her. All the rollicking fun one could ask for lay beneath her canopy, among the behemoth branches. Several groups of children could play at once among her branches and not disturb each other. She sheltered the sand beneath her majestic canopy from the withering Texas sun, keeping the sand soft and cool beneath her. It made the sandbar a delight to play, dig, and wrestle on. But most of all, she made it a pleasure to sleep upon its cool countenance.

We threw down ragged blankets and sleeping bags next to the person that, according to the strict hierarchy of the world of boys, dictated our assigned place. Sometimes it was oldest to youngest, or best friends to least best friends, at times best athlete to least, other times strongest to weakest. There was always an order. I was usually somewhere in the middle of any given group and invariably next to Billy Swift.

A couple of boys gathered wood for a fire. Some began climbing on the mighty branches. So big and strong was the Swiss Family Robinson tree that even the oldest and coolest of the boys respected her. No nails were driven into her to hold up tree forts. There were no carvings upon her, no branches broken for firewood. Some of us went and stood on the bank of the creek. Joey Briggs had a fishing pole and threw a line in. Stevie Walsh unzipped his shorts and began to pee in the creek just upstream from Joey.

"Hey, you peckerwood!" Joey cried. "You're gonna scare the fish!"

"Tough titty said the kitty," Stevie replied casually. "How 'bout some one-eyed trouser trout?" He turned toward Joey, shaking his penis at him.

Some of the younger boys standing off at a distance couldn't take their eyes off Stevie's member.

"Jeez, look at all the hair he has there," said Chris admiringly.

His brother Paul nodded. "His pecker is that long!" he said in a hushed tone, holding up two fingers a couple inches apart.

"That dude's a man."

The growing dusk created magic. A mere thirty yards away lay the closest house, but we might as well have been on our own, exotic island. No sign of civilization could be seen through the thick, surrounding woods. We were on our own; independent, wild, free.

We cavorted in the sand under the glorious tree. We sang made-up songs with dirty words in them, splitting our sides with laughter. We shucked our clothes and jumped en masse into the creek, splashing and diving in the cool water. Skinny-dipping felt like we were breaking all the rules. We were at play in a garden of God.

Bags of chips, Fritos, and Cheese Doodles appeared and warm soda too. As evening lowered the light into dusk we sat on our sleeping bags around a blazing campfire, competing for the loudest belch and vying for the honor of top fake farting noises, cupping our hands in our armpits and flapping our arms up and down. Later, as darkness descended, we practiced making birdcalls the way we saw Indians do in the cowboy movies we watched on TV.

After the last of the wood was consumed and the fire began to slowly fade we lay in our sleeping bags, staring at the fire and talking softly with the ones lying next to us.

"What time do you think it is?" someone said.

Billy Swift looked at his glow-in-the-dark Timex wristwatch. "Almost 12:30."

"Cool. It's after midnight."

Suddenly Stevie commanded everyone's attention. "Let's all beat off and see who reaches puberty first!"

Raucous laughter all around. Some of the younger boys secretly suspected that the older ones had already reached puberty and reached puberty often. Every time they touched their tallywackers, they presumed. After all, didn't touching it feel good?

"C'mon, everyone do it," Stevie commanded.

"I'll do it!" Joey exclaimed. "I know how to reach puberty. I've done it before." He rolled over onto his back in his sleeping bag. Soon a small tent began moving vigorously up and down in the sleeping bag below his belly.

From Chris, "I'm a man! I can do it."

"I'm the only man here," Stevie crowed. He rolled onto his back.

Some of the other boys looked around at each other, giggling. One by one we turned over on our backs.

Billy Swift and I looked at each other with devilish smiles on our faces. Billy giggled. "Let's do it!"

We flipped over onto our backs. I unsnapped my shorts, unzipped my fly, and inserted my hand into my underwear. Lately touching myself in the privacy of my bed or in the bathroom sometimes felt exciting in a way I couldn't describe. It was just this new and wonderful sensation I captured sometimes that made me quiver. I gazed up through the canopy of the tree at the twinkling of stars. It felt nice.

Soon all of us were lost in our own reverie, captivated by the feelings in our loins and the rocketing pleasures of base, physical ecstasy.

"I did it! I did it!" exclaimed Paul suddenly. "I did it! I reached puberty!"

"Nuh-uh," someone said. "Not that soon. It takes awhile. My cousin Peter said so. An' he's in high school."

"Did too!" Paul retorted. "I freakin' reached puberty again!"

He scrambled out of his sleeping bag, clutching his penis in a choke hold. "Look! I can prove it! Feel the end of it!"

He moved around the encircled group. A few of the more curious reached out, touching the end of the wet penis.

"Ewwww! He did!"

"Told ya! Didn't I? Told ya!"

A couple more curious takers. Billy Swift was one. I declined, but I did notice in the dying firelight that the end of Paul's penis was wet. I was still dry myself.

The contest was won. The night belonged to Paul.

We settled back comfortably into our sleeping bags. Silently, we listened to the night noises.

"Is it nighttime in Vietnam right now?" someone asked.

"It's daytime there, doofus. Vietnam's on the other side of the world."

"What do the army guys do at night in the jungle over there?"

Billy Swift spoke up. Being that his dad had been a full bird colonel in the Air Force, he was considered knowledgeable on military matters. He had even lived in Japan when his father was stationed there, which everyone thought was close enough to Vietnam to be an expert.

"They post lookouts," he said matter-of-factly. "They switch up every four hours. They also set up trip wires if the Viet Cong try sneakin' up that set off claymores. An' they wear camouflage, even at night."

"I saw on the six o'clock news that there's a lot more fightin' now," Robbie said. "They're callin' it the 'Tet.'"

"Sounds like 'tit,'" Stevie mumbled from his sleeping bag.

Some of us snorted with laughter.

I thought about the leathernecks over there. They were Marines, and I knew they were the toughest. I wondered what they were doing right now. I wondered if sleeping outside in the jungle was as neat as camping out under the Swiss Family Robinson tree. It was the last thought I remembered before falling asleep under its protection.

We sat around the dinner table in glum silence.

"Really?" Willie bleated. "No fam'ly vacation? Dang!"

Mother picked at her plate, moving the Hamburger Helper around. "Your father won't be back this summer, except for the Fourth of July. Vacation is cancelled this year."

"But we still got the station wagon!" I said. "Why can't we go?"

Mother had already thought of that. All the kids, by herself, for the annual two-week summer family vacation. That vision caused vertigo. Father's company had relocated him back East. The plan was to have her stay put with the kids till the house sold. It seemed so easy at the time. The realtor had practically promised a stampede to the house in this desirable suburban neighborhood in the beginning. "In two months," he said, "you'll be sailing out of here with money in your pocket." That was January. Six months and two realtors later we were still here while Father had remained back East. Real estate was in a slump. The "stampede" of potential buyers was a thin trickle.

Showing the house was a nightmare for the whole family. The realtors pressed Mother on the importance of a house that was spic-n-span before prospective buyers showed up. Mother was promised 24 hours notice. It was usually more like three. She would scramble after working the 7 to 3 shift at the hospital to get home, depending on Eileen to corral us boys into making the home presentable. It resulted in wars, with Mother showing up at home just ahead of the realtor to find one of us boys with a swollen lip, courtesy of another of her daughter's trademark right hooks, two of the other boys nowhere to be found, and the remaining son stretched out on the couch in front of the TV seemingly unaware he had any role in making the house neat. The dog, a high-strung Irish setter, would be jacked with excitement.

A stiff drink became a stable ally. By the time dinner was done, Mother was exhausted, leaving the boys to the chore list posted on the refrigerator in her distinctive hand script, hoping at least some of it would get done.

Bobby, just five, began to cry.

"Stop your crying," Mother said.

"I wanna go to the lake!" he wailed.

"We always go on vacation every year, Ma."

Eileen chimed in. "I don't give a doo-wop about vacation."

"Whattaya mean!" Timmy cried. He wore glasses framed by thick, utilitarian plastic, with a patch over one lens to help correct a lazy eye. It made him look at you with his head at a funny angle.

"I mean that's a another two weeks I get paid to babysit you twerps." she sneered.

"Big woo!" I said hotly.

"Big woo yourself!"

"Your father is working hard for us, and you have no right to complain!" Mother was at her limit and in no mood to brook any more dissent. Her voice rose. "When he calls tonight you will thank him! You will not mention anything about vacation or you will upset him! And that is a sin!"

Silence. The church had been invoked. There would be no more protest.

"I wanna go on baycashin!" Bobby wailed, unwilling to let it go. I was secretly glad. We always went on vacation. Every year. Interminable hours crammed into the Country Squire station wagon with Dad at the wheel and the speedometer pegged at sixty miles an hour. The usual complaints from the back:

"I gotta pee!"

"I gotta throw up! Really!"

"I'm hungry!"

"Bobby's touching me!"

Mother's stock reply: "Be quiet and look at the scenery."

But we had seen the country. From Montreal to Cuidad Juarez.

Vermont to Oregon. And Lake Winnipesaukee. The one constant, it seemed, in what had been a seminomadic life for the family, beginning in New Jersey. The glacier cut, crystal clear water of Lake Winnipesaukee in New Hampshire held a special place in the collective heart of the family. We had slept in a Holiday Inn owned by Mickey Mantle in Joplin, Missouri. We explored Belle Starr's primitive cabin in the Arbuckle Mountains of Oklahoma. We'd walked the hallowed grounds of Gettysburg and the Alamo. Family vacations were the shining achievement for our family. For the first time in family memory, there would be no vacation. It settled on us like darkness as we sat at the dinner table.

Mother looked down at her plate. "Clear the table," she said, almost inaudibly. She got up and left the room.

"Way to go, twerps," Eileen said, glowering at us. "You upset Mom. Hope you're happy. Just wait till tomorrow."

The threat made us swallow collectively. We knew it was not an idle one.

⟹

The synergy created by four boys sharing one bedroom proved a very effective haven of isolation within the home from unwanted trespassers such as annoying sisters and meddlesome parents. The combination of active boys indifferent to bathing (in our opinion swimming in the mossy tank behind our house met that standard), one bed wetter, one given to hiding soiled underwear in the room in futile attempts to evade detection, and all of us comfortable with picking days-old clothing off the floor to wear again formed an invisible, potently malodorous and unsightly force field. Colleen and Eileen steadfastly refused to enter, usually holding their noses and shutting their eyes whenever they passed by on their way to their room. Mother and Father entered only when parental responsibility made it impossible to ignore, which consisted mainly of the regular nighttime belt strapping of all four of us to induce quiet or when someone's underwear kept failing to make its way to the laundry. Only the family dog seemed to enjoy the room's rich atmosphere.

This night, after our mother's announcement, each of us lay in our beds, which consisted of two sets of bunk beds. I, by virtue of being the oldest, had the top bunk next to the door. Timmy lay under me, Willie in the other top bunk along the wall, and Bobby under him, closer to the floor because of his frequent falls out of bed, given the nonstop rough horseplay going on in our room. Silence pervaded in the darkness.

"No vacation," Timmy said dejectedly. "That stinks."

"Yeah, just cause Dad's not here shouldn't mean we can't go on vacation," Willie said. "Mom can drive. She takes us every week all the way to Dennison to the liquor store."

I lay in my bunk, hands behind my head, looking up into the darkness, brooding. Family vacations were a point of pride for me with the other neighborhood boys. Ours was one of the few families in the neighborhood to practice that modern, nuclear family ritual. I often bragged of the places I'd been and sometimes, when friends were over I would show them souvenirs from far-off places. Most of the neighborhood had never been out of the state of Texas. I had been everywhere. Lately, I had made loud proclamations about where the family might be off to this summer. I would wonder aloud about the possibilities. The whole thing was stupid, I thought. I scowled in the darkness. I hated my father for not being around this summer. Heck, he hadn't been around since January. Before he left he said to me, "You're twelve years old now. You're the man of the house." He tousled my hair. "Be good and obey your mother." So far as I could see, being the "man of the house" meant doing more chores than any of my brothers and being the sole lawn mower. *Big deal,* I thought. I hated my mother for cancelling family vacation.

"I'm sneakin' out," I said suddenly. I sat up in my bed.

"Wow!" Timmy said. "Really?"

The sudden declaration galvanized my brothers. This had never even been contemplated before, much less attempted.

"Whatta ya gonna do?" Bobby said.

"I dunno," I replied. "Walk around the neighborhood."

"I'm tellin'," Willie said.

"You tell and I'll beat the crap outta you!" I hissed fiercely. I jumped over to his bunk and landed on top of him, pinning him. I glowered down at him.

"You gonna tell?" I said menacingly.

"Maybe," came the stubborn but wavering reply.

A swift punch to the shoulder followed. "Ow!" came a loud protest.

"Shut up, butthole! I said, are you gonna tell?"

"No," came the whimpering reply.

"Better not." I got up and swung to the floor, landing featherlight. I was now in stealth mode. Years of playing in the sprawling woods and pastures like Huck Finn, tracking animals and playing war, had developed superior abilities in stealth.

Shucking my pj's, I picked a pair of shorts, a dirty tee shirt and socks off the floor and got dressed. Then I found my ratty PF Fliers and pulled them on.

"Keep Bridie from barking," I said. "I'll be back later." I cracked open the bedroom door, stopping just short of where I knew the creaking would start. I slipped out, quietly closing the door behind me. I was now officially in no-man's-land, totally vulnerable to discovery. Being found this late at night fully clothed and sneaking around would be fatal. No excuse would be sufficient or accepted. My mother's retribution would be swift and harsh. The thought of this brought my senses to a fine edge. I felt gloriously alive.

I moved toward the stairs, taking a short step, then one long stride at an angle to the right to avoid a known floor squeak. Quietly, I descended the stairs, avoiding the ones that made noises, and then climbed onto the banister. We often played a game in the house of climbing on the furnishings throughout each room downstairs without touching the floor. The only place in the home we had been unable to navigate was the upstairs hallway. The training came in handy now. I crouched at the back door that led through the utility room. I waited, listening. I heard only silence. Still, I hesitated. Mother slept lightly and had the hearing of a lynx. Being caught now would be bad. But not as bad as being caught outside. Nothing stirred in the house. My brothers were obeying my admonitions.

I opened the door slowly, closed it behind me, and went through the small utility room, past the washer and dryer, and out the back door into the cool, starlit Texas night. The smell of nearby pasture, musty, dark, and rich, filled my senses with the freedom of the pioneers. I walked softly through the yard and around front till I came to the street. Avoiding the streetlight, I stepped on to the cool pavement and broke into a headlong, exhilarating dash. I felt as if I were flying. The entire neighborhood was at my sole command. I was in solitary, all-consuming, Christmas morning, two-pound bass catching and touchdown-scoring bliss.

I ran until too winded to run any farther. Then I slowed to a walk, feeling the beating of my heart and breathing deeply and satisfyingly, inhaling the nighttime scents. I walked through yards and between houses. I walked the entire length of the utility alley behind the parallel row of homes where a town garbage truck lumbered once a week and where the neighborhood boys sometimes careened our go-carts down, hitting the occasional garbage can. Mikey Phillips once ran over the Smith's poodle while racing down the alley, killing it. It was a while before any of us used the alley again after that tragedy. Stevie Walsh hadn't helped matters by asking Mr. Smith if he could take the dead dog home and use it for target practice in his backyard.

The stars overhead formed a fabulous, glittering canopy. Toads croaked in their hidden places. In the distance a dog barked. Nighttime noises had their own, ethereal quality that I marveled over. I wished I could live outside at night always.

Walking between two houses I was suddenly frozen in place, stabbed by the sudden switching on of a light from a bedroom window. I stood rooted to the spot, afraid to move.

Keeping my body statue still, I slowly turned my head in the direction of the lit window. What I saw transfixed me. Allyson Petrie was in her bedroom, framed by the window. The blinds were fully raised. I could not turn away. Allyson was one of the prettiest girls in the neighborhood, if not the prettiest. She was going into the tenth grade. Although she was nice enough, boys like me were invisible to her. She began to undress.

I swallowed dryly. My heart leapt in my throat. I forgot everything, the cool night air, the stars, the croaking toads. Allyson, unaware that she was transporting a twelve-year-old boy to a distant universe, casually continued undressing. Unbuttoning her blouse, she tossed it on the bed. I zeroed in on her bra. I marveled at the wondrous, faint lace. And now, as my heart pounded like a locomotive in a long tunnel, I watched her bend a lithe arm around her back and unsnap her bra. She shook it off, and I entered a place far beyond my vivid imagination whenever Billy Swift and I snuck off to our secret hiding place in the woods where we kept a stash of old *Playboy* magazines. This was the real thing, and it was magnificent.

Allyson stood there for a moment, as beautiful as a statue of any Greek goddess I had ever seen in *National Geographic* or a museum. Then, while I watched agape, she gave her beautiful, teacup-size breasts a gentle, comforting massage in reward for having been confined all day in a bra. The erection in my shorts felt like a stone.

Allyson disappeared from the window and reappeared a moment later wearing a thin nightie. I could see her nipples through the garment. She drew down the covers of her bed, walked over toward the bedroom door, and flicked the light switch off. My night vision was ruined. I could see nothing. I turned my head from the window, still fixed to the spot.

After a minute or two, I began moving again. I walked toward home, the erection in my shorts so hard I walked as if I were limping. Although I consciously could not think why, I knew in a fundamental way now why boys had boners. It was still a mystery, but such mystery never felt so wonderful.

It took quite an effort to return to stealth mode again for re-entry to the house. All the way through the downstairs and up to my bedroom I struggled to keep focused on the task at hand. My mind wanted to return to the wonderful vision I had encountered. My erection was still there. Finally, I was safely back in my bed.

Timmy was still semi-awake. "What didja do out there?"

"Nothin'."

"Didja see anything?"

"Nope."

"Dang, sounds like a waste of time."

I didn't reply. I lay in my bed on my back, dreaming with my eyes open. I fell asleep with a sure choke hold on my tallywacker.

⟫

Billy Swift, Mikey, and I stopped for a rest at the old abandoned dairy. Mikey snapped off some dried grapevine for cigarettes. We sat against one of the curved concrete retaining walls that stood about three feet high and ran down each side of the building, smoking. We were sure it had been a dairy, although no one had ever confirmed this. The ruined building sat in the middle of thick woodland and measured about sixty feet long and forty feet wide. Its crumbling concrete walls had evenly spaced, empty windows with rotted, glassless wood frames. Both ends of the structure had wide openings in them to allow cattle in and out. The roof was long gone. Small trees here and there had managed to take root in cracks in the concrete floor. The middle of the building was wide open from end to end. Near each long wall there ran curved concrete retaining walls and behind them, ancient stalls with enough room to accommodate cattle when their rumps were against the exterior walls. Trash, debris, and scrap wood littered the place. It was a boys' paradise.

We stopped there to tarry for a while after an afternoon of hunting in the woods with BB and pellet guns. I owned neither, though I had been relentlessly badgering my beleaguered parents for a shotgun for the past year. Finally, they struck a deal with me. If I earned my merit badge in marksmanship this summer at Scout camp, they would allow Santa to bring one for Christmas. Until then, I was forbidden to use any firearm whatsoever. That rule ended at our front door. My parents were unaware of it, but I was already an accomplished marksman. There were plenty of boys in the neighborhood who owned firearms ranging from BB guns to .306 deer rifles. When it came to specialty items such as girlie magazines, fireworks, motorcycles, and guns, boys are very willing to share. It increases status among us.

Given the smaller caliber of our present weaponry, we relegated ourselves to hunting small birds and cicadas. Cicadas were especially interesting both for the challenge they presented spotting them in trees and actually hitting one of them, or capturing them alive. Keeping them as temporary pets was fun. If one was good enough to shoot their heads clean off, the ill-fated cicada would emit a long, fading buzz as it fell from the trees.

Capturing cicadas required stealth and effort, as any tree they were in would have to be climbed, the hunter obliged to shimmy out on a branch high above, then slowly, very slowly, reach out to the quarry that had suddenly grown silent and, in a last-second move, quickly strike out and grasp the inch-and-a-half long harmless insect in a hand. Once snared, the captor then had to negotiate the climb back down, with one hand holding a furiously buzzing cicada. After reaching the ground, a long length of kite string would be tied around the abdomen of the insect and the other end around the wrist of the enslaving owner. The cicada would invariably rise in the air in a buzz to the limit of the string and remain there, flying in place, as its captor would walk about. It was a common sight in the neighborhood to observe a boy or two walking about in the street with one end of a twenty-foot length of kite string tied to one wrist and the other end to a cicada up in the air vainly trying to escape.

Billy Swift and I tried riding our bikes around one day with one hand on the handlebars and the other outstretched with one end of kite string tied around a wrist and the other end tethered to a captive cicada flying in the air above us. Navigating our bikes was proving tricky, as we had to keep an eye in the air to prevent jerking our quarry too hard in one direction or another which would kill them, while avoiding running into the curb or each other. At one point we collided. We managed not to fall over, but in our efforts to remain upright, our cicadas became entangled with each other.

"Don't jerk your hand that way," Billy hollered. "You're gonna kill my bug!"

"You're the one who's moving their hand around!" I yelled back.

We climbed off our bikes, watching the cicadas buzzing overhead and bumping into each other. Billy and I continued to yell at each other as we tried to untangle ourselves.

"Turn this way!"

"I am!"

"The other way!"

"Shut up!"

Mrs. Henderson looked up from the flower bed she was kneeling in toward the commotion. She watched with bemusement as Billy and I worked to untangle our lines from each other. She could see we were not going to succeed and that we were becoming increasingly cross with each other.

"You're getting it tangled even more, you butthole!" Billy cried.

"Shut up!" I shot back. "Bring your hand over mine!"

Meanwhile, the two suffering cicadas were becoming more distressed, colliding with each other with increasing frequency and buzzing angrily.

"Stop moving!"

"You stop moving!"

Neither one of us noticed Mrs. Henderson approach. With a deft move, she reached out with her pruning scissors in a gloved hand and snipped both lines where they twisted together near our wrists.

Surprised, Billy and I watched with dismay as the two cicadas flew off in opposite directions.

Mrs. Henderson looked at us as we gawked up at her, squinting in the sun.

"That takes care of that," she said with finality. She turned and walked back to her flower beds, leaving Billy and I staring at her back.

⸺◆⸺

There were three things that mattered most to me. Their ranking depended upon what I was doing at the moment. Of the three things I loved, I loved most the one I was doing at the time.

Football was ingrained in my DNA. From my earliest memory, football was important. It was important to the whole family. Dad had been a local high school football hero in the small New Jersey town he'd grown up in, just over the Hudson River from New York City. His forbearers had landed there from Ireland, coming over in the coffin ships during the famine years. They lived and endured in the immigrant slums of the city, eventually moving into a traditional Irish vocation; the fire department. Before World War II interrupted, Dad played football for Fordham and entertained thoughts of following his father and brother's footsteps into the fire department.

Mother came from an upper-crust Boston Irish family whose

patriarch had been a local football hero before World War I. After their move to the same New Jersey town her future husband lived in, her own brother had become a local high school football hero as well and went on to star at Cornell. She had been a dutiful daughter and sister by hero-worshipping both father and brother.

At twelve, I was very small and so skinny my mother sometimes would tease me, calling me a "beanpole." But I was quick and agile and possessed a great instinct for the game. The highest praise I heard had come from Stevie Walsh, who had been a first-string football player at Dillingham the past three years and looked to be a first-string choice on the high school JV team when school started up again in the fall. During a pause in one of the neighborhood games, he had pointed to three or four of us who were playing and said, "I predict that you guys will be first-string next year on the seventh-grade team." I had been one of those singled out by Stevie. It made me supremely happy inside, though I tried to be modest about it. Nothing thrilled me more than to carry the ball around the end, deke one or two defenders out of their shoes, and light out for the end zone, hair flying. My mind would race as I ran, imagining the television announcer calling the play with excitement. "He breaks around the end. What a move on the linebacker! He's in the secondary. One man to beat. Oh! What a great move! He's off to the races, ladies and gentlemen! He's at midfield! The forty! The thirty! The twenty! The ten! TOUCHDOWN!" In my mind I could hear the crowd at the Cotton Bowl going wild. I would replay that glorious narrative in my mind every time I got my hands on the ball and broke into the open.

Another love was something I had discovered during the fifth grade in the school library. Books. Overnight, I became a voracious reader. There was the biography of Lou Gehrig, chosen at random. Lou Gehrig became my boyhood hero. I admired the quiet strength, humility, and tenacity of the man as he played through every ache and pain a professional athlete could endure, never missing a game until ALS finally felled the giant.

I read a book on the fateful battle at Gettysburg. The Union Army, commanded by Irish/American George Meade. That made me swell with pride. General Lee, revered by the rebels. Joshua Chamberlain, his Maine 20th regiment, almost out of ammo, saving the entire Union Army by refusing to be overrun and countercharging instead. It started a love affair with history. The Revolution, the Alamo, Lewis and Clarke. I read them all.

Books transported me to other worlds. When I picked one up, it became my sole activity till it was finished. I read *Where the Red Fern Grows* three times during my fifth-grade year. I would read the livelong day away, and when time came for bed, I went with my Boy Scout flashlight and continued reading under the covers until I gave up trying to shake light from it as the batteries faded.

My third love was the woods and pastures. They called to me like no other force in the universe. My stomach would tighten in anticipation just walking through the yards until I reached their liberating embrace. I explored every inch of pasture and woodland surrounding the neighborhood. I once asked permission to live in the woods for forty days and forty nights, just like Jesus in the desert. I loved being alone in the woods. I would sit for hours at the comfortable base of a noble old oak, caressing the rough bark, examining every nook and cranny, every feature. I sat in pecan trees, patiently cracking the pecans and eating, feeling like an Indian. The clay earth, so great for making the dirt clods we boys used to hurl at each other during some of our war games, was fragrant with the history of the prehistoric ocean that once lay above it. I inhaled it.

I prowled the creek beds, sifting the gravel in the sandbars for the ancient sharks teeth that I collected and kept in my room. Some were over an inch long, others just a tiny fraction of an inch, probably prehistoric gar and other small predators. But to my friends and me, they were shark teeth.

I would cut through the pastures from woodland to woodland using the cow paths worn deep into the fragrant grasses and bull nettle, unless there was a group of Herefords with their bull watching over them. We had chased enough calves and mothers to know that if the big, longhorned one with the big huge ball sack hanging down was there, you left them alone and stayed along the perimeter of the field, along the barbed wire fences.

I smoked grapevine cigarettes and spied on the secretive and mysterious Woodman Circle Home, a large, foreboding hulk of an ancient brick mansion that lay in a state of disrepair a half mile from the neighborhood through the woods and pastures. Tales of being shot at by the caretaker with a shotgun blast of rock salt for trespassing was an urban legend in the neighborhood. It was rumored that two orphan children, a brother and sister, lived there. No one had ever seen them. Many secret missions were launched from the neighborhood through the fields and woods to the edges of the Woodman property to verify the orphans' existence. From there, we low-crawled through high grasses and shrubs as close as we dared to the main building, hoping to catch a glance of the two unfortunate children. The slightest noise, a car door closing or a lawn mower starting up, created an instant panicked retreat to the safety of the woods and out of range from any shotgun blast of rock salt.

I hunted rabbit and squirrel with my imaginary .410 shotgun, the one I felt sure I was going to get for Christmas. I could track animal footprints, knew what they were, how long they'd been there, and where they were going. I had read about it. I studied tracks. It was only when an animal crossed over a limestone crag or outcrop that I would get stumped, searching the far side to pick the trail up again. When I was able to get my hands on a BB gun or pellet rifle, I would hunt. Only two animals scared me. Tarantulas and scorpions.

Once, I'd been stung by a scorpion. Bending down to pick up a dirt clod to throw at someone, there had been a fat brown specimen lurking underneath. I spotted it, but before I could jerk my hand away, it jabbed my middle finger with its barbed tail. I ran home in a panic, sure that I was going to die. Eileen looked it over, and then told me to get lost. I waited, lurking in the garage till my mom got home and showed her the swollen, discolored finger. Seeing no stinger embedded, she instructed me to have a seat on the couch in the den while she looked it up in one of her medical books. After a while she came back with two Bayer Aspirins and a cold compress for my finger. She told me to lie on the couch. I would be fine, she said. I was sick for two days.

My first encounter with a tarantula had been equally harrowing. Except this time I was a mere witness. My brothers and I and a few others were tormenting a big specimen lumbering across the street one day, poking it with sticks and throwing dirt clods at it. We became curious when we observed it curl its long, hairy legs under its body, like the closing of a fist. We approached cautiously, encircling it. What happened next seemed to occur in slow motion. The huge spider, almost the size of a saucer, suddenly sprang high into the air, scattering the crowd. I watched it as it launched, up and off to the side, just above our heads. It came down smack-dab on top of Willy's head.

A long siren of terror rose in the air as Willy flew into a seizure of panic. He began dancing up and down, madly raking the top of his head with his hands. The tarantula was thrown harmlessly off to the side at the first swipe. This fact did nothing to calm Willy. Despite assurances to the contrary he peeled off for home shrieking and flailing with his hands at the top of his head. It took but a moment for the rest of us to burst into laughter at his expense; glad nonetheless it wasn't any of us. The next time we encountered a tarantula crossing the open street we fetched a long plank and, laying it down on the street with one end trapping the hairy beast under it, one of us walked up the plank from the other end until the loud, thick sounds of a crunching exoskeleton could be heard emanating from underneath. From then on, it was the standard procedure for executing trespassing tarantulas.

⟢

"C'mon, chickens!" Billy Swift crowed as he bounced slowly up and down on the trampoline, twirling the bullwhip in his hand round and round over his head. With a flick of the wrist he popped the whip in the air, creating a sharp snap that crackled in the air. "Bocbocbocboc!" he crowed again, like a rooster.

The rest of us stood ringed around the trampoline, just out of range of the business end of the whip. It was one of those eight foot long, braided rawhide leather ones that several of the neighborhood boys had, purchased from the Texas State Fair in Dallas. It was the genuine article and oftentimes several of us wore painful welts on our backs hidden under shirts from our mothers until they healed.

Billy Swift continued bouncing up and down. It was one of the rules. The one with the whip had to remain continuously bouncing and at a certain height as well to give those on the ground around the trampoline a chance to dash under it where it was deemed safe and off-limits from the whip. The next objective would be to dash from under the trampoline and out of range of the hungry whip without getting popped.

"Higher," one of us called out. "Higher!"

"I'm high enough, chickenshit!"

On the ground we crouched at the ready, gauging Billy Swift's jumps as he spun around watching his prey, twirling the whip. We unconsciously rocked slightly back and forth, timing our mad dash.

Paul broke first for safety under the trampoline. Billy swung in his direction, prompting several more boys to break toward the trampoline. Billy spun sharply away from Paul, anticipating the second wave of boys. The killer instinct gleamed in his eye. Out flicked the whip. It found Robbie's shoulder with deadly accuracy.

"Yeeowww!" came an agonized scream as Robbie crumbled to the ground.

It was the break I was waiting for. I leaped forward, skinny legs driving hard. Seeing me out of the corner of his eye, Billy twisted in midair in my direction. It was a rare, though not unheard of, feat to be able to nail two players during a single go-round. The whip came round in good time to set up the two-for.

But I was crafty. Rather than try to dodge and weave, which amounted to more time being exposed in the open, I had planned my dash with smart strategy. Halfway between the safety beneath the trampoline and me was an exposed part of a thick root from a nearby pecan tree. I reached it within two strides, planted a foot over the root and, using it as a starting block, pushed off against it. The move accelerated my forward momentum, virtually launching me toward the trampoline. The move proved too fast for the whip and as I dove forward to cover, I heard the angry snap of the whip in the space where only a split second before I occupied. I rolled under the trampoline to join the others, triumphant.

"Oh, man!" Billy Swift cried. "I almost had ya!"

"That was close," Paul said, grinning at me as we crouched under the trampoline mat. "Nice move."

I grinned back. "I saw it on *Combat* once," I said of the move. "The sarge had to beat a sniper."

Suddenly Willie came running around the corner of the house into the backyard toward us.

"Dad's home!" he cried. "Dad's home! He's back for the Fourth of July!" He stopped where he was and stood staring at me crouched under the trampoline.

"I'm tellin' you were playin' on the trampoline," he said accusingly. "You're in trouble!"

"You better not," I growled through gritted teeth.

Willie turned on his heels and began to run. I scrambled out from under and began to take off in his direction. A loud crack snapped in the air beside my ear.

"Dang it, Billy," I screamed. "I ain't playin'! Cut the crap! I gotta go."

Billy laughed. "Get outta range then. That's the rule."

I jabbed my middle finger at Billy. "Eat me," I said and turned around to chase my brother down.

I caught up to Willie easily. Looking back over his shoulder as he ran, he began taking his words back with a worried look.

"I'm not gonna tell," he pleaded. "Honest. I ain't gonna tell."

I came up alongside him. A soft punch to the shoulder was all that was required to assure my brother's word. We began walking together. I took a piece of Bazooka bubble gum out of my pocket, opened it and pulled the piece in half and offered Willie the peace offering. I popped my half into my mouth and began unfolding the comic that came inside the wrapper. The comics were kind of dumb, I thought, but I always read the little pearls of wisdom under the small picture frames.

Willie explained excitedly that Dad was back home from New Jersey or Massachusetts or wherever he had been along with Colleen, who had been spending the summer working in Boston and living with grandparents. I adored my oldest sister. She was kind and gentle and nice to me and never beat me up like Eileen did. But my brother wasn't through.

"Dad brought fireworks with him!"

"Far out," I cried out loudly. "C'mon, let's go!" I took off like a shot, leaving the slower Willie fading in the distance, imploring me to wait up.

I flew into the house and found my father in the den.

"Hey, there, Danny boy!" my father called out. He smiled broadly. "How are you?"

I threw my arms around my father's waist in an excited hug. "Ya came back for a visit?" It was not so much a question. "An' ya brought fireworks?"

"Sure did," my father said, regarding me. "Gee, I think you've grown a little. Have you been playing football?"

"Every day!" I exclaimed.

"Great! Gosh, you're still so skinny. You need to start lifting weights. Seventh-grade football starts in September, you know."

"I have been! Me an' Billy together in the guest bedroom!"

"Good for you!"

"Wanna see me throw the ball?"

"After supper. I'm cooking hamburgers on the grill."

"Oh," said I without enthusiasm. Dad's prowess at the grill left a lot to be desired. His hamburgers were like hockey pucks. I had never held a hockey puck, but after years of choking down my father's hamburgers, I knew what they must feel like.

"Are we gonna have fireworks tonight?" My enthusiasm gained new life.

"We sure are," said Dad. "When it gets dark."

"Far out!" I took off to hunt for my football.

After supper all four of us boys sat on top of the picnic table on the small, poured concrete patio behind the house. We were consciously willing the sun to set so that the fireworks could commence. Our family set off an array of fireworks each year in the backyard. Roman candles, whistlers, bottle rockets, and sparklers. For the grand finale each year, our father would set off an entire package of firecrackers. Our dog would go nuts and run into the exploding bedlam, barking wildly, jumping and twisting madly trying to subdue the wild enemy. It made for great entertainment.

Each of us was given an allotment of various ordnance, our parents being careful to be equal to stave off the frequent protests about fairness that exasperated Mother and Father. Being fair and equal with six children was a constant challenge and frequent flashpoint. We kept constant, vigilant score as to who got what and when.

We watched as the blue sky slowly faded toward the reds and oranges that began to paint the sky. In open country like Texas, the sky is so big it seems to come all the way down to the ground. One could feel closer to the sky in open land than if we were on the tallest mountain. It came down so unimpeded I could feel its weight.

The colors began to deepen toward twilight. "Look," Timmy said, pointing to the sky. "There's Venus!" We sat in silence gazing at the evening star.

"Starlight, star bright, first star I see tonight," Willy began quietly reciting. We had learned such rhymes from Mother. The rest of us chimed in. "I wish I may, I wish I might, have the wish I wish tonight." We immediately fell silent as we made our own secret wish.

"What'd ya wish for?" Bobby asked.

"Ya can't tell anybody," Timmy admonished. "Or else it won't come true."

I wished for muscles. I would need them for seventh-grade football and be a star like my dad. I was sure I would be.

At last Father emerged on to the patio, grocery bag in hand. It set off an immediate frenzy of "Me first!" and "I want bottle rockets!" and "Can I light my own this year?"

Father hushed us and set the bag down on the picnic table. He began to pull out the contents and arrange them on the table. We fairly danced with anticipation. Even Colleen and Eileen were excited.

Once all was divided and any squabbles settled, the fun began. Each of us had a long punk, lit off the end of Mother's cigarette. Father kept manageable control over the excited brood as we began to set off our allotted stash. He worked to ensure proper distances and nip any attempt to sneak up behind a sister and light off a firecracker. As usual, the dog was in epileptic seizure.

I took one of my favorites in hand, a seven-shot Roman candle. I loved to hold them out in front of me, the business end aimed toward the trees that climbed the bank of the dam rising up at the end of our backyard. I would always try to get one of the colored, phosphorous rounds through the trees and into the water of the tank beyond. My father lit the fuse for me.

I watched enrapt as the first two rounds went off, orange and then green. Then, it all went wrong. Without warning, the remaining five rounds exploded from the rear of the foot-long cardboard stick in my hand and into my midsection, setting my shirt on fire.

Stunned at first, I stared down at my shirt. It was rapidly beginning to burn in bright, angry colors. Then, I took off, running wildly and raking the front of my shirt with my hands. The dog immediately started running alongside me, barking wildly. Father ran after me. The yard was a standard lot-sized yard, not very big. But in my panic I proved a very elusive target. He ran after me, shouting my name and trying in vain to grab me. To his dismay, I had made leaps and bounds in my agility over the past six months.

By the time Dad was able to grab me and throw me to the ground, the entire front of my shirt had burned away and ugly burn marks were beginning to appear on my skin. The pain was excruciating, and I wailed loudly.

Mother went instantly into command mode. "Get him inside," she said tersely. "Get him into the bathroom and get his shirt off."

Dad picked me up in a bear hug as I flailed and headed through the sliding glass door of the patio. The others watched in horrified silence, the fireworks forgotten.

By the end of the whole episode, Mother had concluded I was going to be fine. "You're going to live," she said simply. The burns, painful though they were, caused nothing more than some blistering and scorch marks. The shirt fared worse, its damage being deemed fatal and so relegated as a rag to the utility room. But it had saved me, as far as I was concerned. I was able to return to the activities in time for the grand finale.

It was the Fourth of July, 1968. The Tet Offensive had sputtered, resumed, then sputtered again, a saga I followed closely on the

Huntley-Brinkley report each evening on TV. There were riots as well, things I didn't understand. I saw people burning draft cards. I saw others, women, burning their bras. I thought that was hilarious. Dumb, I thought too. They'd just have to go to Sears and buy new ones. The television showed large crowds of Negroes, their fists in the air, demanding equal rights. It made me wonder because I thought everybody had rights in America. Not like some commie country like Red China. I thought Iron Butterfly was a great rock-n-roll band, and my friends and I would frequently break into song, singing loudly, "In-a-gadda-da-vida honey, don't you know that I love you...?" And I was now afraid of fireworks.

=◆=

Paul, Chris, Joey, Stevie, and I leaned against one of the retaining walls of the abandoned dairy. Joey was busy trying to clear a jam in his pellet gun. After a few minutes, he fired off a quick few rounds at the remains of a glass bottle.

"Huntin' cicadas is like huntin' niggers," he said as he looked over his rifle. "They're both tricky."

The others giggled and nodded. I knew Joey used a bad word. I'd heard it before. Once, I came into the kitchen and saw my mother fixing dinner.

"Hey, Ma," I had said brightly. "Listen to what I just learned!"

I went on to sing, "In 1944, my daddy went to war. He pulled the trigger and killed a nigger and that was the end of the war."

I finished the little ditty and smiled at my mom, waiting for her laughter.

She swirled around at me. The fury in her face froze me in my place. I had no idea what brought this on but her dark look terrified me.

"Don't... you... ever... use... that.... word... AGAIN!" she spat out.

"What word?" I had replied, trembling. My smile had run away.

"Nigger," she said. "Do you want people calling you 'shanty Irish'?"

"Ummm, I guess not."

"It's an ugly word. Don't ever repeat it. Do you understand me?"

"Uh-huh."

"Everybody is the same, and it's a sin to use bad words about people. Do you understand me?" She fixed me with a penetrating stare.

"Ummm, what's a shanty Irish?"

"It's what they used to call your great-great-grandfather and all the other Irish when they came here."

"Oh," I said, completely missing any connection. "Can I go back outside now?" I beat a hasty retreat without waiting for a reply.

So I ignored Joey, pretending not to hear. The others gathered in the dappled sunlight of the old dairy agreed with him.

"After Martin Luther King got shot this spring I saw some niggers downtown yellin' and stuff," Paul said. "One of 'em was holdin' a sign, but I couldn't read it. It just had, like, initials on it. SCC or somethin', I dunno."

"My dad says hang 'em all," Stevie said. "He's right. I've played against niggers whenever we played Piner Junior High 'cross town. All of you better be glad you're goin' to Dillingham next year," he said knowingly to us who were coming out of elementary school. "At Dillingham, there's only a couple Mexicans and niggers, and they know how to behave. Piner is full of nothin' but niggers, spics, and White trash."

I wondered about that. I had precious little experience with anyone who wasn't White. Maybe Stevie was right.

"When we had football games against Piner, I'd look across the field at the other players and you can't see nothin' under their helmets 'cept big ol' white eyes," Stevie went on. "That's 'cause they're scared of us!"

"Goddamn right," Joey said. "When I get to seventh grade next year, the first football game we play against them I'm gonna smash one right in the mouth!"

I didn't know what to think. I was confused. All I cared about was football. My brothers and I all had Dallas Cowboy football helmets at home and would play endless games in our backyard, claiming the personas of various Cowboy heroes. "I'm Don Meredith throwing bombs to Bob Hayes!" "I'm Bob Hayes!" "I'm Bob Lilly!" "I'm Chuck Howley!" "I'm Cornell Greene!" I had been heartsick for weeks after the infamous "Ice Bowl" up in Green Bay the previous December. I couldn't grasp the connection between this mean talk about niggers and spics and playing football. Still, I was glad I was going to Dillingham. My sisters both went there and knew a lot of the football players. I had seen the school a bunch of times, and it looked swell. I'd never heard of Piner 'til now.

"Do any of the Piner players become Bearcats in high school?" I asked Stevie.

"Some, but they're just benchwarmers," Stevie replied matter-of-factly. "Most of 'em go to Frederick Douglass High, not our high school. Frederick Douglass just plays other nigger schools. They don't play the Bearcats. They'd get creamed!"

I had been to plenty of games at Bearcat Stadium on Friday nights. It was a favorite family thing to do. Almost the whole town came out for the games to watch the local gridiron heroes. It's what Texas did on Friday nights. The atmosphere surrounding the games, both on the field and in the stands, was electric. Even those kids and adults who cared little for the game would come for the social atmosphere of the event. Our little town would pack the stadium six thousand strong every home game. Frederick Douglass, the predominantly Black high school, and the mostly White town high school both used the stadium. Frederick Douglass, however, was relegated to Thursday nights. Friday night belonged to the town high school.

Above all else, I wanted to be a Bearcat. If Piner kids were just benchwarmers for the town high school or went to Frederick Douglass instead, I wanted no part of either. I wanted to play football for the Bearcats and score touchdowns just like Bullet Bob Hayes.

⟪⬥⟫

Hearing several loud voices in the garage one morning finally distracted me enough from TV to go investigate. In the garage I found my brothers and a few of their young friends peering into a large cardboard box that had previously housed a washing machine. They were staring down into the box, talking excitedly. Suddenly, the box moved with a thudding sound. The gathered group jumped back en masse.

"Wow!" one of them exclaimed. "Didja see that?"

"I didn't know they were so quick!" said Willie.

Curious, I walked over to the boys standing around the box. I leaned over to take a look and gazed down upon one of the most ubiquitous animals in the great state of Texas. I had seen many before, usually as road kill along Highway 82. But never this close up. Inside the box, sniffing around in the corners, was an armadillo. They're even uglier up close, I thought. My mouth was agape as I stared at the prehistoric-looking animal.

"Where didja catch that!" I asked, mesmerized. I had tracked them plenty of times before, but never came close to catching one.

"Me an' Randy caught him," Timmy said proudly. "Down by the creek."

"How?"

"With this," Randy said. He held up a large fishing net on a pole. "We were huntin' turtles."

I looked back down at the armadillo. "What are ya gonna do with it?"

"Keep it," Timmy said brightly. "As a pet!"

I regarded the animal closely. It was indeed ugly. Small pink eyes, leathery scaly skin with its distinctive, pleated folds crossing its back, and long, dangerous-looking talons extending from its feet at the end of short, stumpy legs. I was doubtful about its usefulness as a pet.

"Did ya give it a name yet?" I asked.

"No, not yet," Randy said. "I think 'Pedro' is good though."

We pondered Pedro. Someone suggested Clancy.

"How 'bout Elizabeth?" one of them suggested.

"A girl's name?"

"Why not?"

"Is it a boy or a girl?"

"I dunno."

"Have ya picked it up and looked?" I asked.

"Not yet," Timmy replied. "We just dragged it home in the net."

"Pick it up for us, okay?" Randy said to me. "You're the biggest one here."

I felt a sense of pride for being so regarded. Still I was doubtful. Every now and again, the armadillo would make a sudden move in the box. It was quicker than it looked. But, I had my pride.

Carefully, I leaned over the box. Slowly, cautiously, I reached my arms toward the bottom. The armadillo became very still. I steeled myself. Then, my hands pounced down on the animal's dirty back, pinning it. Immediately it began to struggle. I maintained my grip, adjusting it as the armadillo continued to fight. Gritting my teeth, I secured the best grip I could and began to lift it out of the box. The armadillo went temporarily limp. I held it out triumphantly toward the others. They oohed and aahed excitedly.

"Look!" one of boys exclaimed. "He's pooping!"

"Eeeeeewwwwwwwww!" they chorused together.

I looked warily at the animal in my hands. It was indeed pooping. Wet excrement fell to the garage floor. I then noticed that what I first thought was just dirt covering the armadillo was actually more poop, all over it, and now all over my hands. There was a noxious smell as well.

Again, "Eeeeeeeewwwwwwwwwww!"

The armadillo began to struggle again with sudden urgency. I tightened my grip, making the poor animal struggle even more. I began to feel it slipping. Before I could move the armadillo back over the box, it fell out of my hands to the floor. It landed with a plop, scrambled on the concrete floor for purchase, then took off like a shot under the station wagon.

Bedlam broke out. A couple of boys dashed out of the garage and down the steep driveway screaming. My brother and his friend Randy began yelling at me.

"Ya better not let it escape!" Timmy's face was flushed with anger.

Willie and Bobby were shrieking.

"Close the garage door!" I yelled at Randy and Timmy. I tried to see where the armadillo had gone but was afraid to get down on the ground to see all the way under the car.

Randy and Timmy ran to the garage door, jumped, and grabbed the handles and began lowering the large, two-car door. It threw the garage into darkness. Little Bobby ran for the utility room door and opened it to escape. There sat Bridie at the ready, whose hunting instincts were on full alert. She jumped into the garage, barking wildly.

"Somebody turn on the light!" I bellowed over the din. No one complied. I ran to the utility room door, reached inside, and snapped on the light switch. Quickly, I slammed the door shut and turned my attention to the dog, which had apparently trapped the armadillo behind a pile of bikes.

I grabbed Bridie's collar and began to pull her away. It was a struggle. She was a strong, sixty-pound dog. It was all I could do to pull her back into the utility room and shut the door again as she barked.

"Everybody just shut up!" I yelled. "Shut up!"

The yelling died off. "Okay," I said. "Let's just find it and get it back into the box."

With trepidation we began to look for the armadillo. We didn't see it behind the bikes. It wasn't under the car either. We poked here and there without success. Noticing the garage's closet door was open, we carefully peered inside. It was full of boxes, a small workbench, assorted odds and ends, and a refrigerator. It was impossible to see where it might have gone. After a fruitless hour of searching we gave up and wandered out to the backyard. We sat desultory in the hot sun, trying to think of what to do.

Eileen stuck her head out the back door. "C'mon, we're going to the pool." She closed the door.

We looked at each other, not knowing what to do. I decided it. "Guess we better get our suits on." I got up and went inside. The others followed.

The garage door was already up when we came down with our swimsuits on and got into the car. We glanced at each other nervously, all thinking the same thing. What if she runs it over backing up? We remained silent. She started the car, put it in reverse, and began to back up. My brothers and I held our collective breath. No crunching sounds were heard as she backed out of the garage. We peered from the backseat into the garage as the car backed away.

"What're you guys lookin' at?" Eileen asked.

"Nothin'," we answered in unison.

Two days of searching the garage came up empty, although the armadillo was leaving plenty of calling cards behind to let us know it was still around. Mother was beginning to ask what that smell in the garage was coming from.

"I dunno," was the stock answer to everything and anything we needed to be vague about. This was one of those times.

A few days later we were in the backyard playing Frisbee and trying to keep the dog from running off with it. Willie stopped in his tracks while running after the soaring disk.

"Look!" he cried, pointing a finger to the bottom of the earthen dam. "There it is!"

Sure enough, just beyond the backyard where the dam started to rise was the armadillo, rooting around in the weeds.

"Get it!" Timmy cried.

We took off running after the armadillo, which had sensed the danger and scooted up and over the dam. Thankfully, the dog had snatched the Frisbee and trotted off to chew on it, oblivious to anything else.

We scrambled up the dam to the rutted tire tracks on top, looking in all directions. I felt particularly responsible and desperately wanted to find it. There were a couple of neighborhood kids fishing in the tank.

"Did you guys see an armadillo run up here?"

The anglers looked back quizzically. "A what?"

"An armadillo. We had one, but it got away."

"Nope."

My brothers began talking to the kids fishing. I continued to look around for the armadillo. I walked off in the direction of the surrounding pastures. After about fifty yards, I spotted movement in the tall grass. I watched, waiting. There it was, rooting through the field. I took off after it. It bolted, running and zigzagging back and forth in a clumsy, lumbering way. But it was fast nonetheless and before long I found myself deep in the woods and out of breath. The armadillo was gone. I stopped and bent over with hands on knees. Crap, I thought. Timmy would blame me for losing his new pet. I felt responsible. After all, no one I knew ever had such a cool pet like an armadillo.

Regaining my wind, I straightened up. Through the woods I could see the back of the Woodman Circle property. A few outbuildings and a garage and shed stood forlornly behind the main building. I could see a man in a cowboy hat unloading things from the back of a pickup truck. From the safety of the woods I watched, hoping to catch a glimpse of the children. I wondered what orphans looked like and if they had permanently sad-looking faces. After a while I gave up waiting for my chance to be the first to see them and turned for home.

Memory is a curious thing. And curiosity leads to all kinds of discoveries. Discovery creates memories. Curiosity led me to sit on Dolly, a Hereford calf that was more or less a pet of the Cox's, who owned a small ranch across Farm Road 1417 that bordered the world of my outlying neighborhood. The calf wasn't afraid of people like other cattle were, and she would stand stock-still and let you climb onto her back. But that was all she would tolerate. As soon as one was situated, she would buck like the fiercest bull I'd seen at the local rodeos over in Howe. I tried her twice. Both times she had thrown me instantly, leaving me on the ground with assorted bruises and an aching set of testicles.

Curiosity drove my best friend Billy Swift and me to steal a pint bottle of bourbon from my mother's liquor cabinet one day and light off to the woods and our secret hiding place to drink and look at pages torn from a *Playboy* magazine. We were going to be like army men on leave from the war, so we thought.

We sat close together in our little hidden thicket. I opened the bottle and took a sniff. My face wrinkled in disgust.

"Eeeeeyyewww," I grimaced as I held the bottle away from me. "Dang, that's disgusting!"

"Lemme smell," Billy said. He took a whiff, controlling his urge to make a face. He handed it back to me. "Take a swig," he urged.

I hesitantly brought the bottle to my lips. Bracing myself against the sweet, cloying smell, I took a mouthful. Fire exploded in my mouth. Pursing my lips and squeezing my eyes tight, I held the bottle out blindly toward my friend. Billy took the bottle, put it to his lips, and took a mouthful as well.

Both of us looked at each other through watering eyes. Neither of us could swallow the burning liquid in our mouths. Panic started to creep in. I glanced at the bottle. We had taken quite a pull. Rational thought was beginning to elude me. Billy Swift appeared to be having quite a difficult time as well. But instead of just spitting it out, I grabbed the bottle and spit the contents in my mouth back into it. I handed the bottle to Billy, who immediately did the same. We began gasping and coughing instantly. I barely managed to recap the bottle.

"Yaaaauuuugggghhh," I wailed, gagging. My mouth was on fire. "Aauugghh! That's horrible!" I was drooling profusely.

Billy Swift was faring no better. "Wwwwwwaaaaaaaahhhh," was the only sound he could make as he leaned over and drooled on the ground.

We lay there, gasping and spitting and cursing. We vowed never to touch the stuff again. After what seemed an eternity, we collected ourselves and took off for home, parting ways at the barbed wire fence. I went home and snuck the bottle back into my mother's liquor cabinet. I never heard a word about it from her, but the memory of the awful stuff was brightly imprinted upon me.

<hr />

It was the middle of July and my second year of the weeklong Boy Scout camp at Camp Grayson on Lake Texoma was fast approaching. Thinking about it kept me up at night. Unlike some other boys I saw last year crying to go home, I couldn't wait to be away for a whole week in the woods, away from home and stupid chores.

I remembered how great last year had been. Sharing a tent with Billy Swift, being awakened every morning by the scoutmaster and having breakfast in the canteen, braiding lanyards to bring home as souvenirs, cooking over campfires, hiking, swimming, and initiating the unknowing into the world of snipe hunts.

My very first weekend camping trip with my scout troop had introduced me to the snipe hunt. I spent an entire night trying to maintain vigilance, posted in some isolated thicket and told to be patient, still, and quiet, and wait for the legendary, elusive bird. I didn't see one and fell asleep. My scoutmaster found me and several others early the next morning scattered over the fields. He rounded us up and assembled the troop. As I came to know during ensuing camping trips, he gave a short monotone speech about how taking new kids on snipe hunts was against the rules.

By the summer of 1968, I was a two-year veteran camper. Rusty Howard had taught Billy Swift and me lots of neat stuff. This was going to be the best part of summer I thought, especially since there wasn't going to be any family vacation this year. This summer I was going to take some new kids out on a snipe hunt. My memories of camping at Camp Grayson on Lake Texoma were infused with warm, exciting magic. I couldn't wait to get back there.

———◆———

I lurked deep in the green water of the tank, looking up toward the surface. Above me in the prismed sunlight undulating through the water was the wooden raft, floated by six fifty-five gallon drums. It was the quintessential summertime staple for all the kids in the neighborhood. In a time when parents weren't afraid to open the front door and tell the kids to have a great life and be home in time for supper, this particular pastime was that mind-set's epitome. There wasn't a grown-up in sight to watch the kids swimming and playing in the five-acre-sized green water tank overgrown with moss and filled with snapping turtles.

I could hold my breath the longest of anybody. I was very proud of that. I would dive deep, where the sunlight began to run thin and the water got colder, to wait. Just when some of the others were beginning to wonder where I might be, I would slowly rise toward an unsuspecting pair of dangling legs, like the Creature from the Black Lagoon, and grab an ankle. It was great fun, especially if there were girls involved. I could hear their shrieking in ten feet of water.

I floated slowly to the surface, eyeing a pair of legs as I rose. I had no idea who they belonged to, but they were within easy reach. I reached out, grabbed an ankle, and gave a hard tug. In a sudden swirl of turbulence, I found myself being grabbed and pulled violently up. I realized right away it was someone much stronger than me, probably Stevie Walsh. When I broke the surface in my captor's firm grasp my hunch was confirmed. It was Stevie Walsh, and he was spitting mad.

"Damn little shit," Stevie snarled through gritted teeth. "You ever try that again I'll drown your sorry little ass." To emphasize the point he gave me two swift punches to the shoulder.

I put my head down under the water to hide the scream of pain and wounded look on my face. Stevie jerked me up hard, and then pushed me away.

"Little twerp."

I looked at Eileen, who was standing on the raft, for some help. None was forthcoming. Stevie swam over and pulled himself up onto the raft. He and my sister looked at each other, exchanging flirting glances.

"I hate your brother," he said.

"Join the crowd," she replied.

I dove back down, deep. There, I was in my own world. Whether it was in the murky water of the tank behind the house, one of the meandering muddy creeks coursing through the land, or the crystal clear, chlorinated water of the municipal pool, I loved the water.

That love had been born on Lake Winnipesaukee. To me, it was simply the greatest lake on earth. Formed in granite during the last great Ice Age, its crystal clear water, surrounded by the ancient White Mountains of New Hampshire, beckoned me like a dream. Every summer my family would go there, and all us kids would dash pell-mell straight from the car when it pulled into the cottage driveway and splash into the water, peeling our clothes off along the way. One could swim a hundred yards out from shore and still see the sandy bottom, littered with granite boulders. Some were small enough for a boy diving like a dolphin to pick up; some were as big as cars. I loved that lake, just as I had loved the woods and brooks around my house in New Jersey, and now, the woods and pastures of the rolling, gentle hills of north Texas.

And the land loved me. I could feel it. The land played with me as I walked through the wide pastures, flushing grasshoppers to flee in front of me, rising in the air and settling back into the long grass in front of me as I continued to walk, laughing, making the Jiminy Cricket creatures do it all over again, repeatedly.

I felt the love the land had for me, lying alone in the afternoon at the base of a spreading pecan tree, gazing up through its canopy into the endless, azure sky. I felt the embrace of the tank every time I dove off the raft into its warm, then increasingly cooler, depths. The land loved me by sending me jackrabbits to track, grasshoppers to fish with, sharks teeth to mine in the creek beds, and the Swiss Family Robinson tree to climb in. I smoked the land's grapevine, ate the wild pecans, speared horse apples with sharp sticks to hurl at other boys, and inhaled the sweet, musty aromas of the grasses at the edge of America's prairie. I walked in stealth and knowledge through the woods, knowing the birds, feeling the moss, and climbing its trees. I was in heaven, and the land loved me for that.

I poured all of that love into the concentrated wilderness living of Camp Grayson. It was my ideal way of living, in a tent with my friend Billy Swift, curled up in our sleeping bags and listening to the night noises in the pitch-black just outside our tent. At every camping trip I went on I signed up for every activity involving the land and water the camp had to offer. I dug fire pits, scouted the best locations for pitching tents, swam the endurance test in the muddy lake, and spent hours on the firing range with a .22 caliber rifle. I went on every hike, made my own backpack frame like Rusty Howard showed me, and attended the big pow-wows that were conducted every year toward the end of our weeklong summer camp session.

I gathered with all the other boys and watched the pow-wows, mesmerized, sitting cross-legged on the ground with the other Scouts in the firelight after the sun had long set. One of the older Scouts, dressed like an Indian chief, walked regally around the huge bonfire, arms folded across his chest in front of all the gathered boys. Every so often he would stop and suddenly, silently, point to someone sitting on the ground. There were always two silent Scouts behind him dressed as braves. Upon the chief's signal, they would go forward into the gathered crowd and roughly grab the individual being pointed out, lift him to his feet, and drag him forward. The chief would grab the chosen one's hair, lean his head back and mark the forehead with charcoal. He then shoved a pine bough into the hands of the chosen Scout, making him take and hold it. The chosen boy was then pushed roughly to his knees in front of the fire. The chief would continue around the fire, pointing chosen ones out, until there were half a dozen boys on their knees in front of the fire, their foreheads marked in charcoal and holding the pine boughs.

"These are the chosen," the chief intoned in a deep voice. He stood toward the fire, arms raised above him. "They are to be initiated into the rank of Eagle. Let the initiation begin."

With that, colored smoke would begin to emanate from the bonfire, like magic. I had noticed the previous year that when the chief had said those words, a thin wire leading along the ground from the fire through the crowd into the darkness beyond was pulled taut. I knew right away that it was probably tied to a tin can full of colored gunpowder that led somewhere out behind the crowd to someone who pulled it on cue, tipping the can over in the fire. That knowledge didn't matter to me. The ceremony was infused with solemn, earnest magic.

In my first year there, Rusty Howard had been pulled up from the crowd, forehead marked, pine bough thrust into his hands, and shoved to his knees in front of the fire. My heart raced. This was happening to someone I knew. Rusty, along with the other chosen ones, was gone for two days after that. When pressed upon his return to the pack, he was closed mouthed about the experience.

"So what happened?" one of the boys asked excitedly. We gathered around Rusty.

He shrugged. "Nothin' much. Had to camp out by myself with nothin' for a couple of days."

"Really? No food?"

Rusty shook his head.

"No tent?"

"Nope."

"No nothin'?"

"They gave me a canteen full of water and a flint rock. I had to make my own bed out of pine boughs."

"What didja hunt with?"

"I had a pocketknife," Rusty said, shrugging. "That's all."

"Didja trap a rabbit or squirrel or somethin'?" I asked. Visions of survival on my own raced in my head.

"Naw. They gave me a can of Dinty Moore stew on the second day. I ate that an' some pecans."

Rusty refused to go into more detail, saying it was the code of the Choctaw, the Scout troop's chosen creed of conduct, not to disclose the details of the two days of living off the land. The others accepted this with a hushed reverence. Someday it would be our turn, if we earned it. I yearned for that experience.

<hr>

With barely a glance in either direction, Billy Swift and I shot across Western Avenue on our Schwinn Stingray bikes. A blaring horn from a passing Corvair barely altered our course. We flew into the parking lot of the twin Meccas of childhood economic commerce. Situated next door to each other on a corner lot at Western Avenue and Highway 82 was the local Dairy Queen and 7-Eleven store. Any kid with a couple of bucks to spare could have anything his mother didn't want him to.

I thought my bike was the absolute coolest bike in the universe, though I tried to remain modest about it. Gleaming gold in color with a matching sparkled gold vinyl banana seat, the bike shone with chromed wheels and spokes, ape hanger handlebars, and boasted the highest sissy bar in the neighborhood. I religiously waxed the bike with the Turtle Wax my father kept for the family car. On the road or along the cow paths, my trusty steed never let me down. I loved it every bit as much as I loved my dog.

We screeched to a halt in the shade of the overhang that ran along the front of the Dairy Queen and put our kickstands down. Walking into the blasting air-conditioning inside, we bellied up to the counter and ordered our usual, Dr. Pepper and french fries.

Sitting down at a booth with a view out the window toward the 7-Eleven, the next stop on our mission, Billy Swift thumbed through the jukebox on the table.

"You gonna waste a dime on that thing?" I asked. "That's dumb. 'Less you're a millionaire or somethin'."

"I wanna see if they have 'Young Girl' on it yet," Billy replied. "It's a boss song."

"How much money you got for camp anyway?" I was anxious to know. The way my mother was so tight with money I was inclined to believe we were the poorest family in the neighborhood. Kids always had new stuff except us, I thought. She never wanted any of us inviting other kids over for lunch or anything. "It's too expensive," she would say. "We can't afford it." I thought she was just stingy, and it made me very conscious about how much other kids seemed to have.

"Six bucks," Billy said.

I nearly choked on a french fry. "Jeez, you're loaded!" I said enviously. I had managed to scrape together three dollars to outfit myself with candy enough to last the week at Camp Grayson. While all the other boys seemed to have five dollars to spend at the camp store, I never went there with any more than two bucks grudgingly pulled from my mother's purse. It only exacerbated my feelings of poverty.

"How much you got?" he asked me.

"Three bucks," I replied. "Good thing I got those lawn mowing jobs off Stevie or else I'd have nothin'." I chewed on a french fry.

"How much is your ma gonna give you to take?" I asked dispiritedly.

Billy Swift shrugged. He knew I was jealous. He enjoyed the moment of being filthy rich.

"I dunno. Same as last year I 'spect. Five bucks prob'ly. How much is your ma gonna give?"

"Prob'ly same as last year. Two bucks," I said dejectedly.

"They got it!" Billy cried suddenly. "Far out!"

He dropped a dime in the jukebox and punched a couple of tabs. The machine whirred into life; an arm slid down a bar and extracted the selected 45. A needle arm swung into position over the spinning vinyl and descended.

"Young girl, get outta my life, my love for you is way outta line. You better run girl, you're much too young girl..." Gary Puckett & the Union Gap floated out over the place. Billy Swift sang along. I looked glumly out the window toward the 7-Eleven. The DQ stop had already cost me one of my crumpled dollar bills. I calculated how far my remaining two dollars would go.

After Billy had played the same song three times and began drawing irritated looks from the other patrons, we got up and left. We walked our bikes next door. As I swung the door open of the 7-Eleven, Billy plunked fifty cents into my hand.

"Here ya' go, pal," he said with a grin on his face. "Don't spend it all in one place." He walked past me as I gawked at the two shiny quarters in my palm.

"Holy cow, man! Thanks! Thanks a million!"

"Don't mention it," Billy shrugged. He could be very cool when he wanted to be.

"You're my best friend ever," I said unabashedly.

"Yeah, I know," Billy replied, doing a John Wayne swagger down the candy aisle. "You're my best friend too. And you got the weight set so we'll be ready for seventh-grade football."

Together we carefully shopped, maximizing our candy purchases to the fullest. We walked out of the store with two brown bags full of our favorite candy and gum and a small Slurpee to boot. We were expert enough on our bikes to be able to navigate with one hand on a handlebar grip that also clutched the bag of candy and our free hand holding our Slurpees. Together, we rode back down the side streets to where the road met the pastures. There, the trail began that led through the woods back toward our neighborhood.

I was glad I had lucked into three lawn mowing jobs that week, giving me the money for Camp Grayson. Bringing candy was against the rules. It attracted ants and small, foraging animals, and melted chocolate seemed invariably to find its way into clothes and sleeping bags. No one was deterred, however. The scoutmaster tended to keep to himself in his own tent and leave us boys alone in the late afternoon and into the night. If the noise was kept to a dull roar, he let us be. Eating candy around the campfire or using it as currency in the poker games we played in our tents was a camp tradition.

Camp was just a few days away. A few more days till freedom from my bossy sister and younger brothers who always seemed to want to follow my friends and me around wherever we went. Free from having to always be in when the streetlights came on. Freedom from having to be the only one to always have to pick up the dog poop in the backyard.

"I get to go too," Timmy told me as we sat outside on the picnic table. His "So there, how do ya like that?" smugness irked me. Timmy was a year and a half younger and had joined the Scout troop just this past spring. So long as he wasn't a pest and stayed with his own friends, I tolerated his presence at Scout meetings and his attendance at the first weekend camping trip when school let out. But his announcement about the upcoming weeklong camp dismayed me.

"Ma!" I spun around and went off in search of Mother. "Ma!" This seemed unfair to me in the extreme. I had envisioned total escape from my annoying siblings. "Maaa!"

"Too late," Timmy called after me. "She already signed me up!"

I found Mother in the utility room, bent over in front of the dryer.

"How come he gets to go?" I said dejectedly. I knew deep down it was a done deal and no amount of bellyaching was going to change anything. It didn't, however, stop me from lodging my formal complaint.

Mother ignored me.

"Huh? How come he gets to go?"

"Because he's old enough, that's why. There's no reason why he can't go, same as you." Her tone was final.

"But he's a brat!"

"He's your brother. And he can go. You can even help him out while you're there."

"He just better stay outta my way and not bug me is all!" I was hot.

"You will be nice to your brother," my mother growled back at me. "Blood is thicker than water, and you will keep an eye on him. Do you understand me?" She stood up in front of me. She was diminutive at only five foot one. I hadn't yet reached her height, though I was closing in. She was not the least bit intimidated. I was. I moved away, knowing my cause was lost.

I spun and stomped off. "I hate him!" came my exasperated wail. She said nothing.

I went out to the backyard. Timmy was playing with our collection of miniature army men with his pal Randy. He looked up at me.

"Randy's goin' too," he said smugly.

"Big woo!" I shot back as I walked away toward the corner of the house. "You and your twerp friend just better not be buggin' me!"

"Nya nya nya," Timmy and his twerp friend came back, lolling their heads from side to side in unison, sticking their tongues out. "That's just too bad for you!"

I stormed off around the corner of the house, jumped on my Stingray, and went off in search of Billy Swift. We would have to make sure my twerp brother and his twerp friend pitched their tent nowhere near us, and most of all, make sure they didn't find out about the candy stash. With the fifty cents Billy had given me I had bought fifty pieces of Bazooka gum, which would be barely enough for myself for the week, if I was careful. I wasn't about to share any of it with my brother.

===◆===

It was Friday night, supper was over, and some evening skateboarding down through the neighborhood with some of the other boys without any mishaps capped off another full day of the long summer. Reluctantly, my brothers and I straggled in as the streetlights came on, leaving the more privileged ones outside enjoying the twilight. My feet still tingled from the humming vibration created by metal wheels on asphalt that conducted itself from the bottoms of my feet to my scalp.

We were in our bedroom, each preoccupied with our own pursuit. Willie sat cross-legged on the floor in front of Eileen's portable Emerson phonograph with a stack of 45s perched on the turnstile, waiting their turn to drop and play. The sound of the Turtles floated through the room. *"You and me, it's the only way it's got to be. The only one for me is you and you for me..."* We liked the music, frequently joining in on favorite choruses. So long as Willie didn't play too many Beatle songs, which he invariably would do because he was their biggest, most fanatical fan, all of us enjoyed the music. A ritual during car rides to school in the mornings was to sing along with the AM radio all the way to school. We especially loved it whenever "Harper Valley PTA" came on during the morning ride. To us, it was kind of a protest song to all schools. We would all crow loudly at the refrain, *"The day my mama socked it to the Harper Valley PTAaaay!"*

Bobby was playing with a toy truck in his bed, pushing the vehicle over hills of blankets and through corridors formed by folds in the sheets. Timmy and I sat together on his bed, recounting our inventory of clothes and general readiness for camp.

"…Oh, I'm a believer I couldn't leave her if I tried…" the Monkees chirped away in their slick, manufactured tone.

"I don't have seven pairs of underwear," Timmy said. "Even with the ones he gave me." He hooked a thumb over his shoulder to Willie sitting on the floor.

"Just wear some two days in a row," I said low, with an air of conspiracy.

"Really?" Timmy wrinkled his nose. "Mom says we hafta change every day."

"I've worn mine three days in a row before," I said even lower.

"Gross," Timmy said. "Really?"

"Sure. No one checks. Just don't fudge in 'em."

Timmy snorted with laughter.

"Who ya sharin' a tent with?"

"Billy, a' course."

"How do I know I get to share a tent with Randy?"

"Just pair up when we get there and make sure one of you grabs one of the dark green tent bags that'll be in the back of the truck in the parking area. Those are the two-man tents. Don't grab the light green ones. Those are the four-man ones. They'll get mad at ya for that."

"Where do we set the tents up?"

"Just stay with our troop. We all get our own assigned areas. An' don't be too close to me an' Billy."

"Don't worry 'bout it, man. I don't wanna smell your stinky farts anyway." Timmy lifted a butt cheek off the bed and farted loudly. The four of us broke out in laughter.

Bobby looked up from his truck, grinning. "Aw, you let one!" More laughter.

The sound of Eileen stomping up the stairs quieted everyone. When she reached the top we could hear her cursing under her breath. She started down the hallway past our room. All of us stiffened, heads cocked toward the door. She passed by, eyes forward, fists clenched at her side. "God, I hate her," we could hear her muttering. None of us made a sound. When we heard her bedroom door slamming, we exhaled.

"*There's somethin' happening here. What it is ain't exactly clear…*" the Buffalo Springfield's anthem of the times was very relevant to us at that moment. We could hear her in the next room rummaging around.

"Listen," I said. I hesitated, looking at my brother earnestly. Timmy looked at me expectantly. After a moment of thought, I spoke again. "Don't let any of the older kids trick you into a snipe hunt."

"What's that?"

"It's when the older guys take you out an' tell you to wait for a snipe to run by. You're supposed to grab it."

"What's a snipe?"

"A bird. 'Cept it ain't real. So you just sit out there in the dark for hours for nothin'."

"Jeez, that's stupid. I ain't gonna fall for that."

"Yeah, cause I just told ya about it."

"I still wouldn't have done it."

"Yeah, ya would've," I said with a veteran tone. "All the new kids do."

"Did you?"

"Nope," I lied. "Someone told me."

"Who the hell said you could borrow that?"

We jumped. Standing in the doorway was Eileen. She was furious.

"Huh? Who said you could use my record player?"

She moved into the room, covering the distance to Willie sitting front of the phonograph in two strides. He looked up at her, frozen in fear. She reached down and grabbed the record player with both hands. The Grass Roots were letting it be known, "...*In my midnight confessions, when I tell all the world that I love you...*" She yanked the record player off the ground, sending 45s in all directions. The needle slid screeching off the record. Willie was sent reeling over backward. She reached out and grabbed the electric cord of the machine and yanked the plug from the wall.

"It's mine!" she bellowed down at him. She blinked and sniffed the air. "God, it stinks in here." She turned and stomped out of the room, phonograph tucked under her arm, electric cord trailing. Bobby began to cry.

"I hate you!" Willie cried. He surveyed the 45s around him for damage.

I turned to Timmy. "I can't wait till we leave tomorrow."

"Me too," he replied. He sat silent for a moment. "Camping for a whole week is fun, right?"

"It's so boss," I replied with renewed enthusiasm. "Swimmin' in Lake Texoma every day an' all the campfires an' Vespers an' hikin' an sleepin' in a tent an' everythin'."

My brother marveled. He had a dreamy look in his eye. "An' we can stay up late as we want, huh?"

"Long as ya don't bother the scoutmaster."

"Cool."

"An' the best part," I said, keeping my voice low, "we don't have Miss Bossy for a whole week."

We looked at each other with complete understanding.

PARADISE LOST

"...The summer's gone, and all the roses falling..."

The drop-off area by the gates to Camp Grayson was crammed with cars unloading Scouts and camping equipment strewn about. Boys in varying moods ranging from barely contained excitement, those arguing with parents about forgotten items, ones operating with machinelike efficiency, checking their gear for the thousandth time, and the sullen ones, sitting on back bumpers with dark expressions. I knew that the sullen ones were the ones who would be gone by tomorrow. They'd be homesick. I could not fathom that feeling. I thought, *How could anyone not want to be here instead of home?* The entire area was choked in red dust kicked up by car tires maneuvering in the red dirt of the Red River Valley. For me, it was glorious. The whole week stretched out in front of me with no end in sight. I was of the "barely contained excitement" tribe.

There were, in total, ten boys from the neighborhood making the camp. Stevie Walsh was the oldest, being just shy of sixteen; my brother and his friend Randy were the youngest. We comprised most of the members of our troop, which numbered about fifteen. We had subdivided into three packs. The three packs would scout their own campsite within their designated area, thus forming three small encampments that comprised our Indian village for the week.

After the organized chaos of gathering a hundred boys and equipment into our respective troops, we gathered in front of the gates for the camp director's welcome speech. If it was the same as last year, I thought, it would be a recitation of the Scout motto followed by the Camp Grayson theme song. Sure enough, that was exactly how the speech went. When the director finished his remarks, he began to lead the assembled Scouts in grand fashion through the camp song.

"G-r-a-y-s-o-n spells Grayson

Grayson! Grayson!

That's the place where all the Scouts go!

Scouts go! Scouts go!

The man who runs it is a hobo!

Hobo! Hobo!

G-r-a-y-s-o-n spells Grayson

Grayson! Grayson!

That's the place I want to be!"

The gathered mass sang with gusto. Our troop sang the words Stevie Walsh had taught us last year around a campfire one night:

"The man who runs it is a homo!

Homo! Homo!"

We sang our own words with brazen immunity, as the word rhymed seamlessly with hobo, what with a hundred boys and their scoutmasters all singing. Our own scoutmaster, Mr. Turner, gave us a quizzical look, puzzled by our sudden loud chorus, but then smiled broadly at us in appreciation for our enthusiasm. We wildly cheered our cleverness at the song's conclusion. I had no idea what the word meant. I sensed, however, that grown-ups thought it was a bad word. The thought of getting away with saying a bad word in broad daylight in front of adults delighted me. It was going to be a great week.

The troops gathered their gear and headed out along the trails leading in all directions from the camp's entry toward the assigned sites. Our troop, still giddy over our clever lyrical trickery, headed out single file. We hooked a right at the chow hall, a low-slung, rambling brown wood building, and trekked through a small stand of woods into a meadow about an acre in size. It was ringed with scrub oak, mesquite, and cedar trees, the last vestiges of the vast pine forests of east Texas to reach the edge of the Great Plains.

The troop flag was planted in the middle of the meadow. It was both a claim to the land and a challenge to the dozen or so other troops spending the week there to try to steal it. The flag would receive vigilant guard duty from the troop the entire week. It was an ultimate disgrace to have one's flag stolen by another troop. Many attempts on all the flags would be made, both during the day and more stealthily at night.

Billy Swift and I settled on a site and began making camp. Our two-man tent was pitched just into the wood line, with the front of the tent facing the flag in the field. We were part of the first line of defense. We considered ourselves men. We set up our site just like Rusty Howard had taught us; organized and utilitarian. Unfortunately, Rusty wasn't with us this year, as he was attending another camp in New Mexico. But we were determined to show our independence and ingenuity. The candy was stashed in various places around the site as a means of protecting it from total loss, either through another troop's raiding party or discovery by the scoutmaster. If part of the stash was taken, all would not be lost.

Then began the careful, sometimes uneasy blending of priorities between our scoutmaster, Mr. Turner, and the troop. He was orderly, staid, and by the book. We were not. The entire troop was convinced he wore a toupee. Many was the night in camp when we would hide just out of sight around his large tent, which was perched on a wooden platform off the ground, waiting for him to remove it by the light of the lantern as he got ready for bed. So far, no one had ever witnessed it. It didn't diminish our belief however.

The scoutmaster organized the troop site, assigned duties, arranged classes, and kept us on the camp schedule. We were more interested in raiding other troops, playing poker in the tents, playing Capture the Flag, and generally sneaking around at night and frightening the newcomers to camp. It would take a day or so for the troop to find Mr. Turner's boundaries.

That first evening supper was held in the chow hall. Again, as would happen every evening, the camp song. Again, as would happen every evening, our troop rendered our own version in the midst of all the others. Coleslaw, beans, and chicken were served on metal trays. The milk-dispensing machine had chocolate milk. I was in heaven. All my meals would be accompanied by four or five glasses of the sweet nectar I seldom had at home.

The troops sized each other up around the room, looking to see who had the biggest, oldest, and strongest looking boys in their troops. Weaknesses were searched for; who had the youngest, least experienced, or slowest members. Who looked strong and who looked like a twerp. These qualities were noted for further discussion around the campfire back at the various sites later in the evening. I thought my troop fared pretty well in the subtle, subterranean world of the ancient, primitive rite of men and boys in evaluating strengths and weaknesses and ranking each other accordingly. Later that evening there was concurrence on our place in the hierarchy.

The first night around the campfire started as an antsy one for us.

Mr. Turner thought it an important moment in which to bond with his charges. He sat with his pipe on a folding chair, flabby arms draped over a large belly. We sat cross-legged on the ground around the fire. He regaled us with boring stories of past camping accomplishments of his troops in a sonorous monotone that had lost every boy there in the first few minutes.

At last, he wrapped things up. "Any questions, boys?" He looked around the fire at us. There were none. He put his hands down on his knees. "Well, then, I'm turning in." He stood up slowly, knees creaking. His shirt was tucked in neatly, stretched tight across his potbelly.

"G'night, boys," he said, tapping his pipe out on one of the rocks ringing the fire.

"G'night, sir," we chorused back.

"Y'all keep the noise down, y' hear?"

"Yes, sir," we chimed.

Snapping on his flashlight, he turned and walked off into the darkness. We watched, his flashlight moving back and forth as he crossed the meadow toward his tent. At last it disappeared altogether.

"Dang, I thought he'd never leave," Mikey said.

"Damn blowhard," said Stevie.

All of us continued to sit around the fire. The older, more experienced boys talked quietly, the others sat silent, staring into the fire and listening. We discussed our evaluations of the other troops during dinner. It was decided that during the next day when everyone would be moving throughout the camp to various activities that careful notes would be made about the other campsites; the best approaches and escape routes, where the flags were as well as any easy candy stash-raiding opportunities. Results would be shared around tomorrow night's fire.

Later that night, I lay in my sleeping bag in supreme contentment. Billy Swift was snoring softly on his side of the tent. I gazed out of a tent flap into the starlit sky. The Milky Way was splashed softly across the dark vault of the galaxy. My heart quickened at the sight of a shooting star. From reading books in the school library, I knew that Choctaw Indians had lived here a hundred years ago, looking up at the same sky. I felt like one.

The next few days filled me with life. I continued to hone my marksmanship on the firing range. It gave me immense satisfaction. I would leave at the end of camp with my marksmanship merit badge. That .410 shotgun I looked at every day in the Sears catalogue back home was as good as mine at Christmas. My parents had promised.

We hiked through the fields and woods to Lake Texoma and swam in the muddy water. I went to first aid classes in the main gathering field, learning how to properly apply a tourniquet. I wondered what an arm would actually look like that needed one. Pretty gross, I concluded. There was a small open-sided, corrugated tin roof building that housed a small collection of live animals indigenous to the area. There was a rattlesnake in a glass terrarium, a horned toad, a couple of tarantulas, a boxer turtle, a squirrel, and the grandest display of them all; a fox.

I was fascinated by the fox, but felt sorry for him as well. Sometimes when I stopped by, the fox just looked sad and depressed. Sometimes, especially after its owner had given him some Coca-Cola, it acted like a mad animal, snarling and snapping and whirling about the cage. Other boys would dare each other to put a finger in the cage. Looking at the sharp fangs when it bared them, I never considered it.

It was afternoon when Joey came running through the field toward our cluster of tents, yelling for everyone.

"The Longhorns got the Apaches' flag! An' they said they're gettin' ours tonight!"

We gathered quickly around Joey. He sputtered breathlessly that he'd seen a bunch from the Longhorn troop parading back to their campsite with the Apache flag. When a couple of them spotted him, they shouted out that our Choctaw flag was next.

Quickly, scouting details and guard duties were assigned. It was decided that Stevie, being the oldest and strongest, would feign not feeling good and skip supper so that he could remain behind on guard duty. Others promised to sneak him back some supper. We broke off, satisfied we had a plan.

Later, we gathered at Stevie's tent site. Somehow, he managed to have his own four-man tent. Paul and Chris had the tent next to his, and Joey, Robbie, and Mikey Phillips occupied the next tent over. We brought Stevie supper as promised. I pulled a barbecued chicken leg out of my pocket. Billy Swift had one too. Joey produced a piece of corn bread. Paul pulled a soggy wad of coleslaw wrapped in a napkin from the pocket of his shorts. Stevie ate all of it.

"'Kay, this is what we're doing," Stevie began. He looked at Billy and me. "You two are closest to the flag. Watch for flashlights."

"You two," he said, pointing to Randy and Timmy, "you guys watch from the other side of the field."

"Paul, Chris, and Joey, we're gonna put string across the path in case they come that way. We'll tie some cans on the ends to make noise. All you other peckerheads stay around the flag. Make sure you can be seen."

It was the perfect plan. We broke from our huddle like the Dallas Cowboys, clapping our hands in unison and going to our assigned positions. That night, the Choctaw flag flew safe. It was not taken.

<hr />

The next night Stevie hosted the first poker game of the week. I chose not to participate. Last year, in a run of bad luck, I'd virtually lost my entire candy stash to Stevie, Chris, and Joey. I was reluctant to try my luck again. Billy and I sat around our own campfire braiding lanyards to make key chains that would never be used back home. We could hear the goings-on coming from Stevie's tent across the meadow.

"Ya think tomorrow you could show me Five-Card Stud again?" I asked Billy.

"Sure," he replied. "It's just a matter of keeping track of the cards and making a hand you can bet on."

"I got beat bad last year."

"Just a matter of luck is all. Plus you gotta know when to fold. I kept tryin' to warn ya last year."

"Yeah, I know. Shoulda listened."

"Dang!" An angry voice shouted out from Stevie's tent. "Dang!"

Other voices from the tent, hushing. Billy and I looked at each other. "Someone just bet the farm and lost," Billy said smiling. We sat, braiding in silence.

"Ya think the VC can beat our army?" I asked. I followed news from Vietnam on television and in the newspaper regularly. It didn't seem to me that we were making much progress over there.

"Naw, we own the sky over there," Billy replied. "Air power wins wars. That's what my dad says. He should know. He was a full bird colonel."

I knew that was true. Billy's father even had an article about him in the local paper when the family moved into town upon his retirement. "COLONEL SWIFT RETURNS" the headline read.

"Besides, they're commies," Billy said.

I knew that as well. Commies were bad. My mother told me they didn't even believe in God. Not the Russians, not the Chinese, none of them. They were automatically going to hell, she had said.

"Wanna split a Hershey Bar?" I asked.

"Sure," Billy said.

I got up and rummaged through one of my hiding places. I had moved one of my stashes around because ants had found some of my Bazooka bubble gum. I had unwrapped the pieces covered in ants and brushed them off, then carefully rewrapped the gum for future chewing. I wasn't going to waste a single piece. I came back to the fire and sat down on a rock next to Billy. I broke the candy bar in half and gave one to my friend. I looked up into the spectacular night sky. The universe winked back at me with a million twinkling promises. This was the best.

⋯⟨⟩⋯

The next day, I brought back my target from the firing range to show the others. All twenty-five shots were contained within the small, two-inch bull's-eye. Billy Swift counted off each one. Although several of the shots had combined to form one large hole within the bull's-eye and thus couldn't be exactly accounted for, there were no holes anywhere else on the paper. There was no doubt. They had all seen my shooting back home. The perfect score was verified.

"All I gotta do now is take the safety test," I said. "Then I earn my merit badge."

"Far out," my friend Billy said.

When Stevie announced after supper that there was another poker game that night in his tent, I decided to join in. I felt in my bones that my luck had changed. After all, I had a perfect score from the firing range.

Seven of us crowded into Stevie's tent that night. Billy Swift and I sat across from each other. I brought all the candy I was willing to bet with, including the gum the ants had been sampling. I was willing to give those up.

Stevie formed a tabletop of sorts by folding up his sleeping bag and placing it on the floor of the tent in the middle of the group. A battery-powered Coleman lamp hung from the middle of the ridge-pole. The tent flaps had to remain closed to avoid detection from the scoutmaster, creating a stuffy atmosphere. We sat cheek by jowl next to each other in the small space, laughing and jostling each other.

"Five-Card Stud, everyone," Stevie said, holding the deck of cards. "I'm permanent dealer. Everyone antes a piece of candy. Whole candy bars are like, five and ten bucks. They're tops. Gum, jawbreakers, and hot balls are like dimes or somethin'. Milk Duds are the same as a piece of gum. And everyone keep their voice down or I pound ya."

Everyone fished in their pockets and tossed the minimum ante on top of the folded sleeping bag.

"Okay, here we go," Stevie said, smiling like a shark. He'd done pretty well the previous evening, as usual.

Stevie dealt the hands while the rest of us would examine our cards and decide what to throw away or what to keep. The only time four cards could be discarded was if the hand held an ace, which would have to be shown for verification.

We practiced our poker faces, attempted to fill inside straights or bluff our way through many rounds of ante, discarding for new cards, holding, checking, or folding. A full house would be displayed with loud triumph. A winning hand with just a pair of fours was greeted with admiration for the guts to pull off a bluff.

Losers of each hand groaned as they ponied up their candy while the winners would rake each winning pile toward them with glee, exclaiming, "Come to Papa!" or, "Lookit all them Butterfingers!"

Because Billy Swift was a drummer, no one teased him whenever he would exclaim, "Groovy!" any time he won a hand.

The night wore on, arguments ensued from time to time as to which hand beat which and what the limits were on eating the booty as the game went on. Sometimes Stevie's fists settled disputes with quick hard punches to the shoulder. Gradually, the losers gave what they had brought and the winners began pocketing their winnings. After several hours, the candy had been lost and won.

Stevie, who as usual had the biggest pile, wanted to play on. Several of the boys, in particular those with no candy left, wanted to leave.

"C'mon, let's keep playing," Stevie implored. "Tell ya what. We'll play for nothin'. And no discards. Just the hand ya get, straight up."

There was some hesitation, but we all agreed. Stevie began dealing. After several hands, he upped the ante. "Loser of the next hand gets a punch to the shoulder."

Several hands were played, and several punches to the shoulders of the loser of the hand landed with thick, meaty sounds that made me flinch. But no one was willing to be a coward. Everyone stayed.

"Loser of the next hand has to suck my pecker," Stevie said suddenly. A mean grin played on his face. Several of the boys laughed. I laughed too. It was such a silly thing to say. My mind couldn't imagine something like that. It sounded mildly gross, but things had never gotten too gross or overly mean between any of us before.

The loser of the next hand, Chris, threw down his cards. "Okay, man," Stevie said. "Get ready to suck." He got up on his knees and reached for his zipper. Chris said flatly, "I ain't suckin' your pecker. I don't care what you say."

"Fine," Stevie said. "Then you get two punches instead of one."

"I'll take the punches," Chris said.

Stevie leaned over and gave Chris two quick punches to the shoulder. However, they were more like taps. Stevie and brothers Chris and Paul lived next door to each other in the neighborhood. They were friends. Chris hardly flinched.

The next loser was Joey. Again, Stevie kneeled up and this time unzipped his shorts.

"Get that thing away from me," Joey said, holding a hand up in front of him.

"Then have a couple of punches, peckerhead," Stevie said, grabbing Joey's arm.

Joey was also a friend of Stevie's and also received lighter punches on the arm. No one, especially the youngest of us, relished Stevie's punches. But the mood stayed buoyant and lighthearted. There was an unspoken rule among us that no one caused real harm to another. There wouldn't really be any sucking on anything. Stevie's punches could hurt sometimes, but no one was ever killed. Our world knew nothing of such cruelties.

Billy Swift's turn to lose was next. He too refused the invitation to suck Stevie's penis. Suddenly, a change seemed to come over Stevie. He was more insistent that Billy suck his pecker. He unzipped his shorts again.

"Suck my dick," Stevie said through clenched teeth. Billy refused. This time, the punches were hard and furious. I flinched at the heavy sounds as they landed on Billy's shoulder. He slumped over and began to cry in silent pain, holding his arm.

"C'mon, Stevie," Paul said. "Take it easy."

"Shut up and read your cards," Stevie snarled back as he dealt a new hand. Billy was still slumped in tears so Stevie skipped him.

Paul was the next loser. Stevie actually moved toward him and took his pecker out. "Suck it, I say!"

Paul pushed him back. Two swift punches rocketed into his arm. Arching his head backward, Paul's mouth opened in a twist of agony.

"Yeoww!" he cried.

"Shut up," Stevie said. "The scoutmaster will hear us." There was a faraway, mean glint in Stevie's eye. He dealt a new hand.

Mikey lost the next hand. Stevie loomed over him, shaking his penis in front of him. Joey, Chris, and Paul laughed hysterically at Mikey. He actually looked scared.

"C'mon, Mikey," Stevie sneered. "Eat it!"

Mikey looked uncertain. None of them could conceive what putting a penis in their mouth was all about. All we knew is what any of us heard from older high school kids. But all of us knew what getting punched was like. Looking at Stevie's hairy tallywacker though was enough to make Mikey settle for a couple of swift punches. For some reason, this seemed to be making Stevie even angrier. The punches came harder.

Stevie dealt again, including Billy this time. Billy ruefully collected his cards.

This time, it was my turn to lose. I threw my cards down, suddenly afraid. Stevie's punches hurt. I'd had them before. But there was something else wrong here. Stevie was not just being a bully. Something about him was serious. I didn't like it.

"Okay, motherfucker," Stevie said fiercely. He kneeled up and unzipped his shorts again and pulled out his penis. "Here I come." He came across the folded sleeping bag, sending cards flying in different directions.

I leaned backward, reluctantly offering an arm for Stevie to punch. Billy Swift watched mutely, his eyes wide behind his glasses. The air inside the tent was still, hot, and close. It smelled like boy sweat and bubble gum. The lantern swung lightly back and forth, throwing shadows around the tent.

Stevie reached me as I cowered backward and grabbed me by my extended arm. "Enough of that bullshit," Stevie said. His voice was fierce. "I said suck my dick, you little cocksucker."

"No," I said. I was growing very afraid. I'd never seen Stevie like this before. I tried to look away from Stevie's shorts, where his penis, surrounded by a shock of pubic hair, protruded. "No way!"

Stevie rained two quick blows down on my shoulder. The pain exploded in my head.

"I said suck my dick." The same fierce tone of voice. Paul and Chris looked at each other and laughed.

"Look at the little twerp," Paul said with a snort as he rubbed his own shoulder. "He's scared shitless."

"Yeah," Chris said. He was glad though it wasn't him. Stevie was pissed.

Through tears now, I stammered. "N-no. C'mon, man. No."

This time Stevie's fist came down on my chest, knocking me on to my back. He climbed on top and straddled me, pinning me in place.

"Motherfucker, I said suck my dick!" Stevie wasn't concerned about being quiet anymore. He grabbed my hair and pulled my face up to his penis. "I said suck it, little twerp." More laughter from some of the boys, tinged with nervousness. No one had seen Stevie like this before.

My face was screwed up tight with eyes closed and mouth shut. Suddenly Stevie slapped me hard across my face. My ear rang. I opened my mouth to wail.

"Open wide for Chunky!" Stevie sneered. He had a dark mean look in his eyes.

As I started to scream in pain, Stevie grabbed a handful of my hair and yanked my head back. "Shut up and take it, asshole."

With my mouth agape in pain and having my head held backward, Stevie scooted up on my chest and pulled my face forward and directed his penis into my mouth. The others watched in silence. No one made a move.

"That's right, little twerp," Stevie's voice was deadly smooth. "Keep sucking, boy."

He rocked back and forth, moving his penis in and out of my mouth, his free hand holding my head back.

"Look, boys, he's sucking my pecker!"

Paul and Chris pointed at me and laughed. "Lookit! He is!"

Joey joined in the laughter, followed by the others. Only Billy Swift and Mikey were silent.

I gagged. I was trying to breathe at the same time I was trying to expel Stevie from my mouth. I could smell his pubic hair. I felt my gorge begin to rise. Tears blurred my vision. Stevie's penis began to stiffen.

"Yeah, that's right, peckerwood," Stevie crooned. "That's a good boy. Keep goin'."

In desperation, I twisted under Stevie and managed at last to turn on to my side. It forced Stevie to withdraw from my mouth. I stared, bleary eyed, at the floor of the tent. Tears rolled down my cheeks as I drooled and snot dripped from my nose. My ear was ringing. I didn't know if I was going to puke or not. I wretched. Suddenly my face was slammed into the floor as two more quick, hard punches slammed into my back.

"How'd that taste?" Stevie said, retreating to his side of the tent and zipping up his shorts. "Guess we know who the little queerbait among is us now."

Paul, Chris, and Joey laughed. Robbie laughed along with them too. Billy Swift remained silent, an owlish look on his face. Mikey looked down into his lap.

For a moment the boys watched in silence as I sobbed with my face pressed to the floor of the tent.

At last Mikey spoke. "I quit," he said. "It's late." He stood up with his flashlight.

"Yeah, me too," Robbie said as his laughter subsided.

"Guess I'm going too," Billy said quietly.

"Take the queerbait with ya," Stevie said. He was breathing hard.

"Yeah, get him outta hear before he snots everywhere," Chris said. He laughed again at me. "G'night, queerbait."

I stumbled out of Stevie's tent behind Billy into the darkness. When we reached our tent Billy and I undressed without a word and crawled into our sleeping bags. I cried softly to myself, aching with equal pain in my heart and my body. Through tears I looked out at a sliver of night sky framed by an open tent flap, unknowingly mourning the death of my boyhood. Overhead, the stars glittered mutely. Dread lay in the pit of my stomach like a cold stone. It would be with me for a long, long time.

The next morning I woke groggily to the voice of the scoutmaster, who made the rounds to the tents each morning, banging a stick against a tent pole to rouse us.

"Time to get up," he said banging his stick. "Police the area and get ready for breakfast."

I looked out through sleepy eyes at the bright morning light. For the briefest moment, everything looked and felt as it should. It was morning time in camp. Then, with a crushing weight, everything suddenly crashed and vanished. Nothing was the same, and things would never go back to the way they were. I didn't want to leave my sleeping bag. I lingered there till the scoutmaster returned to check on stragglers.

"C'mon, Danny boy," he said. "Let's go!"

Slowly, I climbed out from my sleeping bag.

"Jesus, son," Mr. Turner said, eyeing the blooming bruises on my back and shoulders. "What happened to you?"

I mumbled a reply.

"What?"

"Capture the Flag after dark," I managed. My mouth was as dry as the red dirt beneath me.

"Oh," came the reply. "I'm going to have to have a talk with you boys about that. I can't be sending boys home looking like you. Parents will think we abandoned you in the wilderness." He chuckled to himself and shook his head. "C'mon, boy. Time to eat." He turned and walked away.

I was very sore. Moving slowly, I pulled on some clothes and stood at the entrance of the tent. Billy had already left. I didn't want to step outside. If I stepped outside now, it would all be different. If I stayed where I was, maybe I could delay that inevitability.

My kid brother and Randy ran by the tent.

"C'mon," Timmy called. "Breakfast time!"

Breakfast time was a treat for my brother and me. No plain cornflakes or Cheerios here. Here, we could have French toast and chocolate milk every morning if we wanted. Now I didn't care. I did not want to leave the safety of my tent.

Slowly, with a sigh, I stepped forward, moved a tent flap out of the way with my hand, and stepped outside into the bright morning light. I looked to my right, where I heard voices. Chris, Paul, Robbie, and

Joey were coming up the trail. They looked up at me.

The look in their eyes said it all. It was the end. Of what, I knew not. I felt very alone. The way the others were looking at me told me so. Whatever I had been yesterday, before last night, was dead and gone. I had no idea what I was today or where my place was in the world. I only knew something was lost. Something I didn't know how to name. Something special. I looked at the ground. For the first time in my life, I couldn't feel the earth loving me back.

I lost interest in everything. I never showed up for the gun safety test to complete my marksmanship merit badge. I didn't join in with the others during group swimming periods in the lake and lay alone on my sleeping bag during the Indian ceremony at the bonfire for Eagle Scout initiation. I sat in silence during meals, looking anywhere but in the faces of my fellow campers. Billy Swift and I barely spoke to each other. I spent my time alone in my tent, weaving lanyards.

=◆=

I didn't argue for the front seat when my mother arrived to pick my brother and me up at the end of the week. Perhaps she would have given that unusual behavior more thought had it not been for the wound up, tight-as-a-drum antics of Timmy. When all the gear had been loaded into the back of the station wagon and we headed out onto the dusty two-lane blacktop, my brother could not contain himself. His first experience at camp had been a rousing success. Almost the entire way home he regaled my mother with a virtual play-by-play of his week.

As we pulled away, I glanced back over my shoulder through the rear window of the car. Everyone who'd been in Stevie's tent that night was standing in a group staring at the back of our car. Looking back at them I knew two things: that I'd been forsaken, and that I would never go back to summer camp.

"An' then we had kick ball against the other troops. An' an' an' then we did an Indian ceremony. An' then the next day we paddled canoes in Lake Texoma. An' we had French toast every mornin' for breakfast," and on and on my brother went.

Mother nodded from time to time, occasionally adding an "Uh-huh" here and there. It was an hour ride home. He talked the whole way.

Occasionally she glanced in the rearview mirror at me as I sat slouched in the backseat, staring out the window.

"Did you have as good a time as your brother?" she asked, looking at me in the mirror.

"Yeah, I guess so," came the short, quiet reply.

"An' then guess what?" Timmy plowed back in. "We played Capture the Flag! Me and Randy were scouts! An' then guess what? We went hikin'…" and on and on.

<hr>

The next morning I woke up and came downstairs in my pajamas. All of my clothes from camp were washed and folded on the couch in the den. I went in to the kitchen for a bowl of cereal. It was back to reality. No more French toast and chocolate milk every morning. I sat by myself at the dining table, Bridie beside me. I rubbed a soft ear. She looked up at me in appreciation. She had missed me. I gave her a wan smile.

I didn't have much ambition. I wasn't anxious to get outside. Being without TV for a whole week kept me planted on the couch in the den, next to my clean clothes, watching by myself. I wondered vaguely if *Dialing For Dollars* had tried calling the house. After that, it was *Gilligan's Island*. After that, *Gomer Pyle*. After that, *That Girl*. I kept watching until I was hungry again and ventured into the kitchen to hunt for lunch. As long as the TV was on, I could disconnect from the world around me and the open wound in my soul.

On a morning a few days after I returned from camp I sat lost in front of the TV when Eileen came in from the patio, blowing a last puff from her cigarette back over her shoulder through the open sliding door. "C'mon, get dressed," she said. "We're goin' to the pool." She headed toward the stairs.

Ordinarily I would have stripped naked on the spot and run off to find my swim trunks. The municipal pool was Olympic size with three diving boards. One of the boards was a high dive I had conquered a couple of years before. There was a snack bar and top 40 Rock-n-Roll blared from the loudspeakers all day long. I loved the place.

Now, I wondered if I would see anyone from the neighborhood. Sometimes I did, sometimes I didn't. I walked over to the living-room window and looked out at the neighborhood falling away from the house. Our house commanded a great view, situated at the top of the long, gentle rise. The street heading down from my road started directly in front of my house and gave a view all the way to the bottom of the neighborhood. All the boys I played with, who had been on the camping trip and had been in Stevie's tent, lived along that road. I didn't see anyone.

It was no use trying to argue with my sister. She brooked no disagreement from her brothers. I dug my bathing suit out from the pile of clean laundry and went upstairs to change.

At the pool I hung along the side in the water away from my brothers and watched people jumping off the diving board. Some were really good, doing backflips and gainers and preacher seats. The ones who did good preacher seats made huge splashes. I desperately wanted to go off the diving boards. I could do flips off all of them. But getting up there would expose myself to the crowded pool. Everyone would know I was there. If there was someone there who'd been at camp and knew what happened, or worse, was in the tent that night, then everyone would surely know what happened and would call me a queer. I had no idea what queer meant. I just knew everyone thought it was bad.

I glanced at the clock on the wall of the building housing the locker room and snack bar. There was only a half hour left till my sister came to get us. As usual, she had dropped us off and zoomed off with some high school boy in the front seat. I wanted to go off the diving board. Still, I clung to the side of the pool, occasionally diving underwater where I could truly be alone. The water felt good.

Finally, with ten minutes left before I would have to leave I could stand it no longer. I climbed out of the water and walked slowly toward the diving boards with my head down, studying the cement. I fell in behind a line of dripping swimmers for one of the low diving boards. I stood there, looking down at the ground and stepping forward as the line moved, shivering in the breeze. Finally it was my turn at the steps to the board. I climbed up and stood, looking out over the water deciding what to do for a dive. I was getting good at one-and-a-half forward flips. I glanced over at the line for the high dive. There in line was Billy Swift. He didn't see me at first. I wanted to look away, but couldn't. Then, he turned my way and saw me. I gave a quick wave. Billy returned a terse smile, then turned his head away.

"Hey, kid," someone behind me in line said. "Sometime today, huh?"

I ran and jumped, came down on the end of the board, then sprang straight out in a simple dive. I wanted to get away from there. I swam as far as possible underwater, which was considerable. When I came up I saw no sign of Billy.

TV became a tranquilizer. For days after my return from summer camp I sat numbly in front of the set, staring. If I didn't like what everyone else was watching in the den I would retreat to the solitude of the downstairs guest bedroom and watch the small black-and-white TV in there.

The only time I spurned TV was during the afternoon soap operas. I watched throughout the mornings, then retreated to my room or entertained myself outside in the backyard during the afternoons. I would resume my perch on the floor of the den in the evenings, beginning with the evening news. I was captivated by the news and was a regular watcher with my parents each evening. So far this year, I thought, it seemed the news had been big indeed. North Vietnam launched the Tet Offensive in February, and almost every day the news was filled with reports of fighting in strange-sounding places like Hue and Khe Sanh. In April, Martin Luther King had been assassinated in Memphis. Just after school let out for the summer, Bobby Kennedy was shot in a hotel kitchen in Los Angeles. A Navy nuclear submarine sank in the Atlantic. I shuddered when I thought about all those men drowning in the deep, lightless waters of the ocean. There were riots everywhere it seemed. Washington, D.C., Kansas City, Baltimore, and Chicago.

At the beginning of August, the Republican National Convention in Miami dominated the news. I was captivated by the festive atmosphere and goings-on. When video of the floor of the convention was televised, I marveled over the signs designating each of the states of the country positioned in their places on the convention floor. I always looked for the sign for Texas, as well as New Jersey because I had lived there too. I watched as the people on the floor, with their hats and noisemakers and unbridled enthusiasm, extolled Nixon and the Republican Party. I thought it looked like great fun. I wished I could be there.

"Ma, who are we votin' for?" I asked one evening.

"Nixon, of course," she replied.

"How come?"

"Because he'll fix the country," Mother replied. "It's going to ruin with all these hippies and kooks burning their draft cards and the riots and everything else."

"How will he do that?"

"Because he's a law-and-order man," my mother replied with conviction.

After the pageantry of the Republican convention, I looked forward to the end of August when the Democratic convention was going to happen. Whenever the Huntley-Brinkley Report came on, I was in my spot in front of the TV. But what I saw of the convention in Chicago confused me.

For several nights in a row, I watched as the nightly news and special reports that frequently interrupted regular broadcasting of the events in Chicago unwound. I saw policemen in formation beating people with nightsticks and shooting tear gas canisters into the crowds. I saw people throwing Molotov cocktails, crowds chanting in the streets, politicians and dignitaries issuing edicts and calls for calm. I knew this was very serious. I became glued to the events. The TV showed fires and people bleeding. Within the convention hall, the same circus atmosphere on the floor with signs designating the various states and people acting as if they were at some great party. I watched as a man approached the floor microphone and proclaim that the "great state of Texas casts its vote for Hubert H. Humphrey!" I was proud.

"Hey, Ma!" I shouted from my spot on the floor of the den. "What about Humphrey?"

"Tsk, tsk!" my mother replied from the kitchen. "Another kook. God help the country if he gets elected."

"What's so bad about Humphrey?"

Eileen walked through the den and paused, watching the TV. "Hear that?" she said, pointing at the boisterous street crowd on the television screen. "Hell no, we won't go! Right on, baby!"

Mother appeared at the entry to the den. "You back your country, right or wrong," she said evenly.

My sister turned to her. "Hey," she said defiantly, "if you're old enough to fight, you're old enough to vote!"

"You mind your tone, young lady," Mother said curtly.

I watched silently on the floor as my sister and mother locked horns once again in a contest of wills.

"Get out of Vietnam now!" Eileen shouted provocatively.

"If Vietnam falls," Mother said, "every other country will fall too. Better fighting the communists over there instead of over here!" Her temper was up.

"Bullcrap," my sister retorted.

"If this was a communist country you wouldn't even be eating the Hamburger Helper we're having tonight!" Mother's voice rose. "You'd be eating nothing but rice! And you wouldn't be able to go to church!" She was now visibly shaking.

"Big woo," my sister said. She strode out of the room, leaving Mother sputtering to herself.

<hr />

When television couldn't provide the necessary distraction, I haunted my backyard. I was uninterested in venturing out into the neighborhood, riding my bike, or playing war. I found enough to do there and at the slope of the dam that rose at the end of the yard. My father had landscaped the slope with railroad ties for easier climbing up and over to the tank. It made for a good place to play. The dam itself was heavily wooded on the side facing the backyards of the homes that ran along its length. A large oak was situated directly behind my house, halfway up the slope that made for excellent climbing. I whiled away the hours engaged in different activities, enough to keep me occupied. Apart from the regular football games with my brothers, I wasn't much interested in seeing any of the other boys in the neighborhood. None of the other kids were inclined to venture up toward my end of the neighborhood, except when they would pass by on their way to go fishing or swimming.

I played with my collection of army men in the dirt or fished in the tank, catching the usual crappies and bluegills, hoping for the elusive bass we occasionally caught. I climbed in the oak tree and started a tree house project in it. I managed to construct a small platform, with enough room for perhaps two or three boys, out of scrap wood rummaged from the garage.

I didn't mind my brothers joining me up in the tree, except for Bobby, who I deemed too young to climb that high. We sat on the platform and engaged in idle talk that went from subject to subject. Bobby would remain on the ground, whining to come up.

That first week back from camp I regarded Timmy warily and was on guard trying to discern whether he knew of the night in Stevie's tent. After a few days I was able to relax a bit, convinced he had no inkling of anything. Apparently he and his friend Randy had spent the week at camp caught up in their own rapturous world.

One afternoon the three of us sat up in the platform in the tree, talking and nonchalantly executing small army men by flicking them off the platform one by one.

"You are an enemy soldier," Timmy said, trying to affect a deep, authoritarian voice. "You are hereby executed." With that, the toy figure was placed on the floor of the platform and flicked off the edge with the snap of a finger.

"AAAAAAAAAuuuuuuuuuggggggggghhhhhhhhh," Timmy intoned as the soldier fell to the ground below, fading off toward the end.

"You are a spy," Willie said. "Good-bye." *Flick*. Off went another.

"You're a queer!" said Timmy to a soldier. "Off you go!"

I flinched as if I were punched. I stared down at the soldier I was holding in my hand. I felt my face flush. A question, *Who knows?* screamed in my mind. I continued to stare at my toy soldier.

"Aren't ya gonna execute your man?" Willie asked.

"I don't feel like playin' anymore," I said. I stood up without another word and went to the simple wooden rungs I had nailed into the tree for a ladder. I climbed down without looking back at my brothers.

Once on the ground Bobby stopped whining. I smiled down at him.

"C'mon," I said. "I'm gonna practice kickin' field goals. You can catch the ball."

Bobby brightened instantly and ran off to find the football. After a little while Timmy and Willie climbed down from the tree to join me taking turns kicking the football off the tee.

"No time left on the clock," Timmy announced in the voice of a TV commentator. "He lines up for the kick. Here's the snap. He gets it off. It's going, going... does it have enough? Yes! Yes! It's good! The Cowboys win! The Cowboys win!"

Being the oldest I could kick the highest and the farthest. My kicks were always good, unless I seriously shanked one off to one side or another. In those cases, there was always a penalty called by an imaginary referee that would allow a do-over. I always made the second one. It never failed to buoy me, and this time was no exception.

"Do ya think they kick field goals in seventh-grade football?" Timmy asked.

I thought about it. "I dunno. For extra points maybe."

"I'm gonna go watch the games with Mom when you're playin' for Dillingham to see if they do. I'll bet you'll be one of the kickers!"

The mention of Dillingham froze me. It was August. School would be starting up just before Labor Day weekend, a couple of short weeks away. Dillingham. Where every other boy in the neighborhood would be going, I realized with a dawning dread. Here in the neighborhood it was easy enough to be alone. The sudden thought of me sitting right next to one of the boys in a class who'd been in the tent that night nauseated me.

"I'm going inside," I said. I turned and walked off.

"But it's your turn!" Bobby protested.

I shrugged. "I'm tired. I'm goin' in." I opened the sliding glass door and went in. Eileen was on the couch watching TV. I walked straight through to the downstairs bedroom and flopped on one of the twin beds. I reached over and snapped on the small television set and began to fiddle with the rabbit ears for better reception. I glanced out the window and looked down the street at the neighborhood. I could see Chris and Paul riding their bikes. They were both headed to Dillingham with me when the school year began.

⊷⬥⊶

Alone in my bedroom, I reached into the back of my shelf of the chiffarobe and pulled out the Rand McNally atlas. I lay on the floor and opened the large book to the well-worn pages of Texas. I examined the route I had painstakingly traced for two years in pen and pencil, fingering the line into West Texas and bending south toward El Paso. I thought of how the land looked gazing out the back window of the family's Country Squire station wagon during a vacation trip around the state. Wild, outlaw land that stretched to the horizon. I remembered wandering the grounds of Fort Davis, an isolated outpost during the Indian wars in Big Bend National Park that reminded me of the fort on the TV show *F Troop*. Once we saw wild horses, Mustangs, pounding across the scrubland in a cloud of dust. I had gazed upon the elegant promontory of Mt. Guadalupe, the highest point in Texas.

I looked down now at the atlas, remembering the scenes from our trip. We saw everything. Lubbock and Amarillo. El Paso and Juarez. Houston, with its Space Center and Astrodome. San Antonio and the shrine of Texas independence, the Alamo. San Jacinto, where a wounded Sam Houston, another man of Scotch-Irish descent, had accepted Santa Ana's surrender. Austin and the capitol building. Dallas and the Texas State Fair.

I sighed. I was a daydreamer with too many dreams. I sensed now a crossroads, a choice between competing dreams. Get serious about playing seventh-grade football or get busy getting to Juarez and making my living in the Rio Grande alongside the other boys I'd seen there. In the end, I couldn't leave my family. I argued, fussed, and fought every day with my siblings and hadn't seen my father for the better part of a year, save for the Fourth of July. Eileen was a tyrant, but was also fiercely protective of us. I feared no one in her presence.

Colleen, who I adored, was in Boston for the summer. I missed her. My brothers exasperated me, but I knew them too. They were safe. My family was safe, and I was safe with them. In a neighborhood that had suddenly become an uncertain place for me, my family was certain. It occurred to me that life on the Rio Grande was a little too far and a little too uncertain. Right now, I wanted certainty.

I folded the atlas and got off the floor. I looked at my shelf in the chiffarobe, lingering for a moment. Then, tucking the atlas under my arm, I went downstairs, through the den and the utility room and into the garage. I walked over to one of the metal garbage cans along the wall, lifted the lid, and stuffed the atlas deep inside. I replaced the lid and went back in.

I'm gonna play football, I thought to myself. Right now it was the only thing making sense in my life. Playing in the yard with my Dallas Cowboy helmet on made me forget everything. I was a star, the hero of the fourth quarter. The backyard held me safe. I could be whatever I wanted to be, but most of all just someone who hadn't done a bad thing and got called queerbait for it. I hadn't been back to the sacred woods and pastures since I got back from camp. I hadn't felt like going anywhere outside of my own backyard.

And yet, the earth is a patient mother. Although my world had collapsed inside my heart, the sight of the barbed wire fence marking the neighborhood's end, the wide-open blue sky and the wildflowers waving in the wind and painting the pastures seeped back into my mind, calling me. I found myself more and more simply standing in the backyard, gazing into the distance. One day in late August, standing still and dreaming of the horizon, I simply broke and ran. I ran for a long time. I did not stop until it felt as if my lungs would burst. I stumbled to a halt. I leaned over gasping for air with hands on my knees, my mind gratefully blank.

After a few minutes I straightened up and looked around. The forest's familiar feel and smell reminded me of something I suddenly realized I'd been missing. I began walking, watching the birds and feeling the sun through the trees. Cicadas buzzed overhead. It felt comfortingly familiar. I came to the edge of the woods and looked out over a pasture. Splashes of bright color, bluebonnets and Indian paintbrushes, waved gently in the breeze. It smelled like hay, manure, and cattle. I stepped forward, releasing a horde of grasshoppers that rose in front of me. I smiled and breathed deeply. The sun-warmed scents of the pasture settled familiar into my senses. The breeze lifted the hair off my hot forehead. I looked down at my bare feet and felt the ground underneath. The earth loved me. She had been waiting. I closed my eyes and felt alive for the first time in a long while.

"...If I am dead, as dead I well may be..."

Looking out the living-room window I saw my brothers on their bikes riding in the street at the bottom of the neighborhood, where the street curved left and out of sight. Several other kids were also on their bikes. Impulsively, before I could stop and think, I was out the door and on my bike, heading in their direction.

The bike felt great underneath me. I was always careful to keep the wheel bearings well lubricated. It hummed effortlessly down the street toward the others. Mine was the most boss bike in the neighborhood. My spirit rose on the wind blowing in my face.

Boys and girls were riding around aimlessly, chatting and calling to one another, popping wheelies or making quick starts to build speed and then executing a skidding, sideways stop and admiring the tire marks left on the asphalt. Occasionally a couple of boys would take off in a sudden race. The morning air was bright; the sun had not yet begun its temperature rise to the point in early afternoon that had everyone retreating toward shade.

I rode around with the others, laughing and dodging the other bikes. My bike gleamed in gold. I rode into the alley, up a few houses and turned around. I saw Billy Swift lugging a garbage can to the edge of his driveway. I coasted to stop alongside the edge of the alley at his driveway.

"How's it goin?" I said.

"It'd be better if my mom would quit buggin' me to do everything," Billy replied crossly.

I nodded knowingly. Poor Billy had only sisters. No brothers. He always had to do all the chores.

"That's crummy," I said sympathetically.

Billy shrugged. "Well, I'm done now," he said brightening.

"Whatcha been doin'? Ain't seen ya around." I looked at Billy, wondering.

Billy shrugged and looked away. "Nothin'. Buildin' some models 'n stuff."

"Oh. I was just wonderin'. Ya haven't been comin' up to lift weights or go fishin' in the tank or anythin'."

There it was. Billy knew what I was getting at. Since camp ended several weeks ago we hadn't hung out once. Billy had been caught in a no-man's-land I didn't understand since we got back. The night in Stevie's tent scared him badly. Stevie had been meaner than he'd ever seen him before. He had felt sorry for me but had no idea what to do about it, so he avoided me and now his friend was asking him where he'd been.

He shrugged again, looking at me. "I dunno. It's been weird down here. Stevie, Paul, an' Chris an' everybody else just keeps sayin' you're just a queerbait an' anyone who's your friend is a queerbait too."

"I'm *not* a queerbait!" I said fiercely. I looked around to see if anyone was nearby, keeping my voice low so as not to be heard by the others riding around.

"Yeah, I know," Billy shot back. "Whadda ya want me to do, beat 'em all up or somethin'?"

"Do ya say anythin' to them? Ya could stick up for me or somethin'."

"Once I said that Stevie made ya do it. They just laughed an' said none of them did it. They said it was your own free will."

"Yeah, right," I said sarcastically. "Like I could really do somethin' about it."

"Another time I said at least you're a good football player. They laughed at me an' then said just wait till everyone on the team at Dillingham knows you're a queerbait."

I recoiled as if shocked by electricity. I stared at Billy as I felt my world crumbling around me. I was ruined.

Billy watched me uncomfortably. After a moment he said, "Um, ya wanna come in an' build models with me or somethin'?"

I didn't hear him. The noise in my head was too loud.

"See ya," I said, barely audible. I stood up on a pedal and pushed down hard and took off.

"I'll come up sometime to lift weights," Billy called after me. He received no acknowledgment. He watched me ride away.

I rode past all the others, cut between two of the houses that lined the outside of the long, horseshoe shape of the neighborhood to access one of the many trails that led off into the woods and pastures. I rode hard through the fields, wanting to just disappear from everyone. I rode into the woods at breakneck speed, skimming over roots, dodging trees and low branches and jumping small creeks. I rode and rode, seeking escape. It didn't come.

By afternoon I was hot, sweaty, and tired. I hadn't had anything to eat or drink since breakfast. My father had told me over the phone to make sure I ate a lot while I was lifting weights so that I would grow and get bigger. I felt empty physically and spiritually. The dream I had chosen was going to be killed the first time I stepped into the locker room at Dillingham. From a rise I sat still on the seat of my bike and looked through the treetops over the rooftops of the neighborhood. All joy had left me. I leaned forward over the handlebars. Tears came, falling drop by drop off the end of my nose onto the thirsty ground.

After a couple of hours I emerged from the woods alongside the backs of a few houses. I leaned forward, concentrating on getting past the back of Paul and Chris's house as fast as possible, where the trail led back toward the street. As I rode by I saw Mikey Phillips bouncing up and down on Chris and Paul's trampoline by himself.

"Hey!" Mikey said, calling out to me. "Whatcha doin'?"

I stopped my bike. "Nothin'. Jus' ridin'."

"Wanna play 'Add-on' with me?"

"Where's Paul an' Chris?"

"They went to the 7-Eleven for some RCs. They said I could keep jumpin'. C'mon!"

I was doubtful. I felt better being alone, though even that didn't feel very good either.

"C'mon," Mikey said, smiling a toothy grin. "I can't play 'Add-on' alone. C'mon!"

I studied Mikey's face. There seemed to be nothing suspicious about his invitation. He didn't seem to be hiding anything.

After a moment's hesitation I got off the bike. "Okay," I said. The trampoline was an irresistible draw. That my mother had forbidden it made it more so.

"You go first," I said. I was good at this game, and knew I could keep up with Mikey.

Soon we were locked in heated, friendly competition. After two matches, we were tied at one each.

"Best two out of three," Mikey said.

"'Kay," I said. "I won last one so I go first this time."

I hopped up on to the mat and began bouncing, thinking of my opening move, which Mike would have to replicate, then add another move. Then I would go again, repeating my move, then whatever move Mikey had added, and then add another. And so the game would continue, turn by turn, and add-on by add-on, until one of the contestants failed to complete the string of moves in correct order.

"No backflips!" Mikey said. "I can't do those yet."

The rubber match began. Each of us had several turns. The competition ramped up. This was the championship. We laughed together and talked during the match about television, compared the merits of RC, Coke, and Pepsi, and debated the Kingsmen's mysterious words to the song *Louie Louie*. The game began to get long, making the sequential moves more and more challenging.

I was bouncing up and down with my turn on the mat. Mikey and I were talking over the sequence so that there would be complete agreement prior to beginning my turn. Then the sliding glass door at the back of the house opened up. Paul and Chris stepped outside, 16 ounce RC bottles in their hands.

"Hey, queerbait!" Paul called accusingly. "Who said you could play here?"

I stopped bouncing immediately and stood rooted on the mat staring wordlessly at Paul and Chris.

"Huh? Who said? Get outta here, queerbait!" Paul and Chris started advancing toward me. "Get outta here! Sic 'em!"

I turned and jumped down off the trampoline without a word and headed for my bike. I could feel myself growing smaller and smaller as they continued to taunt me. Mikey stood silently alongside the trampoline, his face wooden.

I jumped on my bike, swung it around, and rode hard back to the safety of the woods without looking back. It would be a very long time before I ventured down into the neighborhood again.

A BRAVE NEW WORLD

"…And when you come, and all the flowers are dying…"

Timmy barged breathlessly into the bedroom. I was lying on the floor reading my *Sport* magazine. Every Christmas I received a yearly subscription. I thought it was the best magazine ever. Looking up at him, I recognized the look on my brother's face instantly. The look defined the cat that ate the bird. Timmy wore the expression that said he knew something big and heralded great news.

That expression had my attention. "What?" I asked quizzically.

"You're goin' to Piner," Timmy blurted. It was news so big he wasn't even able to tease me with any hemming and hawing or other delay tactics such as, "Oh, nothin'."

I jumped from the floor. "What?"

"Mom said you're goin' to Piner. Just now. She's in the kitchen."

I flew out of the room and down the stairs, barely touching any of them. I ran down the hall through the den and hooked a sharp right into the kitchen. My mother stood at the family dining table, looking down at some papers in her hand.

"I'm goin' to Piner?" I asked, incredulous over the prospect. My head was reeling.

"It appears so," she answered, looking down at the paperwork. "Apparently there's been some redistricting. Every student on our street going into junior high, which at the moment I believe is just you, is headed to Piner. Everyone else in the neighborhood," she waved the back of her hand toward the neighborhood that fell away from the front of our home, "is staying put at Dillingham. Huh."

She put the papers on the table, walked over to the counter, and opened a cupboard. She regarded the contents within, planning her supper menu. I watched the back of her beehive hairdo.

"Ya mean they can just split the neighborhood up?" I asked. I was still trying to grasp the implications running through my mind.

"Looks like it," she replied absently.

"Why?"

She turned around to look at me and shrugged. "I don't know. I guess they need to balance things out. The letter says something about integration and that too many families on our side of town were requesting Dillingham. The government will give the town money to build a new high school. But first they're making the town integrate the junior highs. So, the school board decided to send some of the kids on our end of town to Piner instead of Dillingham."

I slumped into a seat at the table. Mother noticed my mystified expression.

"Don't get upset because you won't be playing football for the blue and white," she said, frowning. "And it doesn't matter if all your friends will be at Dillingham. You'll make new friends. I'm sure there are a lot of nice kids at Piner. So no moping, please."

"Huh?" I said from my fog.

"I said no moping. Piner will be just as fine, I'm sure."

"What's their school colors?"

Mother hesitated. "I'm not sure," she said. "You'll have to ask your sister. She went to the games."

After supper I sat outside by myself at the picnic table on the patio. The turn of events from the afternoon ebbed and flowed like tides inside me. It was almost too big to grasp. I knew nothing of Piner, save for the disparaging remarks I heard from time to time from the older neighborhood kids who went to Dillingham. Both of my sisters attended Dillingham before moving on to the town high school. I'd been to Dillingham games. They excited me, even if they didn't measure up to the high school level. Blue and white dominated everywhere I looked in the stands. My sisters wore blue and white pep rally ribbons on their blouses. I would listen as they talked about the Dillingham gridiron players they worshipped. It was magic for me.

Now, it would be a new school I had no reference point for. I racked my memory of Dillingham games I'd attended, but apparently I never went to a game when they played Piner. I wondered what Piner's colors were. I sat at the picnic table, pondering the day's news.

Eileen opened the patio door and stepped outside. I tried to ignore her in case she had something mean to say. She came over beside me and sat down. I regarded her warily. Ordinarily, my sister had little to do with me, unless I was causing her some grief.

Earlier in the summer, before Scout camp, Timmy dared me to do something to the pack of cigarettes she'd left behind while she was at a boy's house up the street. She kept her cigarettes in a fancy, fake leather cigarette case. It was on the dining table, safe from Mother so long as she was at work. Being a nurse, Mother's work schedule was predictable. Eileen often took advantage of that fact with the visitations back and forth between our home and the houses of the high school boys that lived nearby.

I took a pair of tweezers and carefully extracted some tobacco from the end of one of the cigarettes and set it aside. I tore the head off a couple of matches and stuffed them inside the end of the cigarette. Then I carefully replaced the tobacco, tamped it into place, and put the cigarette back in the pack.

A day later, the phone rang. I picked up and immediately heard

Eileen on the other end, calling from a boyfriend's house up the street. She was livid.

"Did you do something to my cigarettes?" she said in an angry, accusing voice. I held the handset away from my ear. She was almost spitting through the phone.

"Whadda ya mean?" I said, affecting an innocent tone.

"Did you do something like put match heads in the end of one of my cigarettes?" Her voice was almost a physical force.

"Maybe," I said, looking skyward, eyebrows raised. "You're not supposed to be smokin', ya know. You know what Ma said." I was feeling very superior. I had the high moral ground. My sister and mother had a running argument over the summer about her cigarette habit.

"You little butthole," she spat through the phone. "Who the hell do you think you are?"

I smugly launched into a brazen lecture about her errant ways. It's a funny thing about the world of twelve-year-old boys, something that affects their ability to weigh action and consequence. I felt perfectly safe taunting my sister in the comparative safety of distance via the telephone. I went on, listing the litany of transgressions she had been committing over the summer that our mother knew nothing of. The list was long, and I was enjoying letting her know my brothers and I were wise to her errant ways.

As I was going on, the front door exploded open. I didn't pay much attention. Loud noises were common in the house. I had stretched the long cord of the wall phone deep into the kitchen, lost in my pontifications.

Angry hands suddenly grabbed my shoulders and spun me around. My eyes flew wide open, surprised to see Eileen's enraged, contorted face up close against me. Mouth agape in midsentence to the sister I thought was on the other end of the phone, I dropped the handset where it fell, clattering on the floor.

"Not so brave now, are ya?" she smiled menacingly down at me as she grabbed me by the front of my tee shirt. "Ya little shit."

She came around with a haymaker and dropped me to the floor. Then she stood over my cowering, crying form. "Don't EVER mess with my butts again, ya hear?"

So, when Eileen crossed the patio and sat down at the picnic table beside me, I was guarded. She seemed calm enough, but I remained at the ready for a hasty retreat.

"Heard ya hafta go to Piner," she said. Her voice was quiet and sympathetic.

"Yeah," came the simple reply.

"Too bad. They're Dillingham's archrivals, ya know."

"Really?"

"Well, yeah. 'Course they are. They're the only other junior high in town."

"I thought Dennison was our rivals."

"That's high school, twerp." She punched me good-naturedly on the arm. "Are ya bummin' out about it?"

I shrugged. I had very secret thoughts about the situation that I couldn't share. I wouldn't have been able to. What had happened to me at Scout camp was beyond my ability to understand, much less talk about. I only felt things. I did, however, understand very well the implication now between me, the neighborhood boys, what happened at camp, and its consequences in the neighborhood. The abrupt change in schools suddenly altered my outlook about the impending school year. I was enormously relieved, as if I were granted a last-minute stay of execution like Luke Cage, my favorite comic book hero. Luke Cage was a death-row inmate who volunteered for chemical experiments conducted by a mad scientist at the prison. The experiments went terribly wrong and transformed Luke into a superhero. He broke out of prison and was now much sought after in his new role.

I sensed a chance for a new start. That realization breathed new life into an aching heart. I understood why my sister and anyone else would be sympathetic. The neighborhood's loyalties were firmly with Dillingham. All the neighborhood kids would view my reassignment to Piner as the ultimate tragedy. I was going to the rival school. Out of that loyalty, friendships would be severed.

I felt they already were.

"Can't do anythin' about it, I guess," I said, trying to sound more dejected than I was.

Eileen put an arm around my shoulder. "Don'tcha worry. I'll deck the first one who says anythin' mean to ya 'bout it. It ain't your fault."

I actually managed a genuine smile for her. "Thanks."

"No prob," she said, getting up. "No one screws with my brothers." She started to go back inside.

"What's Piner's colors anyway?" I asked.

"Green and white."

"What're they called?"

"The Wildcats." She opened the sliding door and went in.

I sat where I was, looking toward the setting sun. Wispy clouds were paintbrushes sweeping graceful, arcing orange and purple brush marks across the Western sky.

Wildcats, I thought. Sounded good enough for me.

⎯◈⎯

The halls of junior high were indeed a whole new world for me. My first day of school was also the first time I'd ever laid eyes on my new school. I had seldom been on the side of town Piner was on. It looked nothing like Dillingham, where I had often been either with Dad when he dropped my sisters off for school, one of their football games, or at one of Dillingham's track meets, conducted on their own track and field behind the school. My brothers and I would sometimes entertain ourselves playing football on the school's practice field that was neatly lined just like a real gridiron. Dillingham was on the west side of town in a nice suburban neighborhood. The school was well kept and modern looking, situated on an attractive campus with wide, mowed lawns, neatly kept athletic fields, and a long canopy that ran along the front of the school to provide shelter for the students on rainy days.

Piner, on the other hand, sat like a brooding hulk in an old-town neighborhood that spoke of faded glory and a future that promised nothing more. Built in the early years of the twentieth century, Piner had once been the town's high school until the late fifties, when the new, modern, and predominantly White high school was built adjacent to the football stadium. The school was a squat, three-story L-shaped, tired-looking brick building with a small, sparse asphalt playground surrounded by a chain-link fence that contained rusty basketball hoops. The school's football teams were bused to an unused field on Centre Street to practice on. The field looked like an afterthought, with a pair of leaning goalposts planted in long, uneven grass at either end of an unmarked gridiron. It reminded me more like some of the pastures surrounding my neighborhood. The coaches used small orange cones to mark the sidelines with. There were no facilities or bathrooms.

I entered the school, clutching a three-ring binder containing lined paper, pencils, an eraser, and something new for me; ink pens. They were a new requirement, and I considered them very grown-up. In my other hand I held a piece of paper with my homeroom number and a map of the hallways leading to it.

I didn't know a single person; yet, despite any trepidation about being in a strange place among strangers, I was fascinated. The halls were teeming with life and noise. Kids of every race, creed, and ethnic extraction were laughing and calling out to one another. One could tell right away who the new seventh graders were. We were the ones looking at our maps in bewilderment as we wandered the hallways looking up at room numbers posted above the doors. Teachers monitored the hallways, shooing kids along and giving directions. I saw two Oriental kids and wondered if they had escaped with their families from Red China. There were Negro kids walking together and shaking each other's hand in a manner I never saw before. I passed a group of Hispanic kids. I was both nervous and exhilarated at the same time. I'd only seen Negroes and Mexicans before from the backseat window of the car when I was downtown.

But the most impressive-looking students, to me, were the upperclassmen. I saw big, strong-looking boys I knew had to be football players and girls that looked all grown-up and positively dazzling. These upperclassmen walked the hallways with a sense of ascendency and importance. I was in absolute awe of them.

I found my homeroom and entered, self-consciously looking for a desk to sit down at. The teacher, an older-looking, lean man sat at his desk checking an attendance sheet. I sat down and peered around the room, looking at the variety and color of the other kids. I noticed something else as well; a couple of cute girls. A big, older-looking Hispanic boy sat down at the desk next to me. He had on a leather jacket with an upturned collar and a perfectly neat, slicked back head of jet-black hair. He oozed cool. I stared unabashedly. He ignored me and sat there, slouching and looking bored.

A bell rang and the teacher set the attendance sheet down on the desk and stood up. "Good morning, boys and girls," he said by rote. "My name is Mr. Clarkson, and I am your homeroom teacher for the year. Welcome to junior high school."

With that, I began my new life. Changing classrooms with each subject was a new experience. Noticing those who I shared two or three classes with was comforting. I found having at least one thing in common with some of the others, such as sharing the same classes, was a natural icebreaker. I was very shy, mousy, and small for my age. I made my way quietly along the edges of the hallways.

The cafeteria was equally fascinating. There, all the kids from all three grades ate at the same time. I would sit, usually by myself, and watch the upperclassmen. They seemed so grown up to me.

The menu also contained foods I'd never experienced at the all-White elementary school I went to on my side of town. Here, there were collard greens and okra, which I devoured, fried rabbit and squirrel too. And corn bread! I'd seldom had it before and loved it. The only new food I encountered I didn't like were the black-eyed peas. I couldn't stand the mushy pile of the brown bean-looking things with the black spot on them. My face screwed up in a knot whenever they were plopped on my plate in the serving line.

Sitting with Tommy Waldron, who was on the football team and in my homeroom, one day at lunch I watched as two ninth graders, a boy and a girl who looked very much to me like brother and sister, sat down with their trays at a nearby table.

Tommy noticed me looking at them.

"Those two kids are twins," he said matter-of-factly. "Bobby and Roxanne Dube. They live out on Route 82, near your place."

"Yeah?" I replied. "Where? I ain't never seen 'em before."

"The Woodman Circle Home," Tommy said. "They're orphans. Folks say their parents were killed in a car crash when they were babies."

I almost choked. "That's them?" I said incredulously. "Really? Those are the two kids who live there?"

"Yup. My older brother James is best friends with Bobby. He hangs out there with him all the time."

Thunderstruck, I regarded Bobby and Roxanne. *So it was really true,* I thought. There really were orphans at the Woodman. The proof was right in front of me.

"Are there other kids who live there?" I asked, mesmerized by the two siblings.

"Naw," Tommy said. "They're the only ones. James says it's just them and their guardians."

The idea suddenly occurred to me that I was the keeper of a great secret. I knew the answer to a mystery that had captured the imagination of all the kids in the neighborhood. We all wondered about and talked of the orphans at the Woodman, but no one was able to claim they had ever seen them. And here I was, going to school with them! They looked quite ordinary to me. I realized since I was the only one from my neighborhood who was sent to Piner, I was the sole proprietor of this sacred knowledge. I knew in that moment one other thing as well. I would keep this secret. No one from the neighborhood would ever know. I looked at the twins. *I will protect you from them,* I thought. In that moment I felt a small sense of victory.

After lunch, outside on the blacktop, I discovered the wonderful game of Foursquare. And always, there was the richness of color, styles, and smells of body sweat and perfume from the other kids. The brilliant sun lighted and mixed swirling colors and shadow into constant motion on the wings of youthful exuberance in front of my eyes. I remained on the periphery, though, gliding along the edges of a slipstream of playful laughter, wanting so much to be swept up, yet constantly afraid of being singled out and called hurtful names.

Late that first week during homeroom, Mr. Clarkson handed me a note and hall pass for the office. I took the note and left, experiencing a virtually empty hallway for the first time. It made me feel very small. I passed other homeroom classes, peering in as I walked by, fascinated by the kids. I found the office and opened the door. I stood there nervously looking around.

One of the school secretaries looked up from her desk as I came in. She shot a sideway glance at her counterpart sitting at the desk across from her. I watched as the other secretary, a large, Black, and warm-looking woman, returned her look. I heard her say something to her coworker as she rose from her desk.

"Looky there at the runt of the litter," I overheard her say. "You could knock him over with a feather." The other secretary giggled.

"Step over here, young man," the large woman said to me. She wore a wide smile on her face that reached her eyes, making me smile in spite of myself.

I walked over and handed her the note. "Ah, yes," she said. "We have your file right over here." She walked over to a table and picked up a folder, checking the name.

"These are your records. They arrived here from Dillingham this morning. You were originally assigned there before the school board changed things," she explained. I listened quietly. She removed a form letter from the folder and placed it on the counter. "If you would, just give this form to your parents, okay?"

"Okay."

I reached across the counter for the form, standing on tiptoes. She regarded me with that same warm smile.

"Thank you," she said. "You're all set, sweetie."

"I didn't know I was comin' here," I said softly.

"Well, welcome to Piner, young man," she said. Her smile grew even wider. "We're glad you're with us."

Impulsively, almost to myself, I said, "That makes two of us." I turned and walked away.

───◆───

Junior high school wrought upon me a most unexpected learning experience, one which all of my male classmates were subterraneously experiencing at the same time, though I was unaware of any but my own tortuous and yet exhilarating predicament. Girls became more and more of a distraction I could not ignore. As the hormones of adolescence ricocheted through me with their hieroglyphic messages I didn't understand but obeyed, I struggled along with the others to navigate the landmarks and landmines of the early teen years.

During the seventh grade, erections, unbidden and untimely, proved a daily challenge to manage without embarrassment. In any given class during the day I prayed not to be called upon to stand in front of the room to read a book report or write something on the chalkboard. At least when the bell rang I would be prepared enough to rise from my seat with my books held in front of me or have a jacket tied around my waist. It confounded me. The slightest provocation, catching the eye of a cute girl, seeing a short skirt, or more thrilling, stealing a glance all the way up a skirt, set off a swirling sensation in my body that instantly made me hard as a rock. It was maddeningly difficult to control. I fidgeted often at my desk. All the boys did.

Junior high introduced me to another rite of social passage, the Cotillion dance, a vestige of the Antebellum South clung to by the dominant Southern White culture. In junior high, there were four Cotillion dances each school year, one at the beginning of the year, two over the winter, and one in the spring. They were the highest social event of our junior high school lives.

My first inkling that there was something special about the Cotillions came during homeroom the first week of seventh grade. The upperclassmen's excited behavior toward the Cotillion dances filtered down, infecting the seventh graders. High anticipation preceded the first exercise of this time-honored ritual, the handing out of invitations.

I sat at my desk and watched while one of the cutest girls in the whole school, Leska Evans, walked up and down the aisles, silently reading the names on the envelopes and handing them to the students. Not every one received one. I wondered if I would suffer the humiliation of being passed over. As she was passing by my desk reading a name on an envelope, she almost walked by, causing my heart to sink. I tried to look disinterested. She stopped abruptly, turned, and handed me an envelope. She looked directly at me and gave me a quick pirate smile that caused yet another instant boner. I shifted in my seat as she continued.

The invitations were the real thing. Embossed and printed in flowing cursive, an invitation with my full name on it that asked me to join with my classmates at the Civic Auditorium downtown for a Cotillion dance. I stared at my name. It was real. I'd been invited.

It was the day before the first Cotillion when I realized with sudden fear that I had no idea how to dance. I'd seen people on *American Bandstand* dancing, but I had never even attempted it. My brothers and I always thought dancing was ridiculous. I didn't think so any more. I sought Colleen, home now from her summer in Boston for her senior year of high school.

Putting a few 45s on the phonograph in her bedroom, she showed me how to keep time to the music, snapping her fingers to the beat. Then, she showed me a few simple steps.

"This is called the 'box step,'" she said. I watched her feet describing a four-sided box on the floor as she danced. "You can do this on any song."

"Whatta ya do with your hands?" I asked. I felt very awkward.

"Anything you want," she replied brightly. "Some people like to do this." Colleen made a rhythmic motion with her hands. "Some people do this." She made circular gestures with her arms. "I do this sometimes." She made yet another motion. She made it look so easy. I made a few clumsy attempts to copy her.

Colleen was very patient and didn't laugh. "That's right. Keep practicing. Good, good," she encouraged.

The next evening, Colleen walked by the bathroom and saw me fidgeting with my tie in front of the mirror. I had a sport coat on that was a bit big, a hand-me-down from cousins back in Jersey.

"Oh, hey," she said sweetly. "You look sharp!"

"Thanks," I said self-consciously. I smiled in spite of my nervousness. I started to leave the bathroom. Colleen looked me over appraisingly.

She suddenly stopped, her mouth open. "Didn't you wash your hair?"

"Yeah, a few days ago. Monday or Tuesday, I think."

"Oh my God," she said appallingly. My hair was an oily slick plastered to my head. "That was *four* days ago! You absolutely can't go like that."

"But it's time to go!"

"You cannot go like that," Colleen said adamantly. She stood there, thinking. After a moment she said, "Stay right there." She disappeared down the hall into her bedroom.

Right away, she came back with an oval container of facial powder. She opened it and lifted out the soft, cloth applicator. "Take off your jacket and hold still," she advised. I did as I was told.

Colleen plopped the applicator down a couple of times on top of my head. A cloud of powder rose above me. She put the container down and mussed the powder through my hair with her hands, grimacing at the feel of my oily mop.

Then she stood back and had a look. Grabbing a towel, she rubbed as much of the powder from my head, face, and shoulders as possible. Finally, she stopped as I was becoming more and more antsy.

"That'll have to do," she said, resigned. "Comb your hair and let's go."

In the car Colleen occasionally snuck a quick look-over at me as she drove me downtown to the Civic Auditorium. My hair was comical looking. It was now puffy and dry. In the soft evening light I could see traces of powder on the shoulders of my sport coat reflected in passing streetlights. I felt nervous and out of place.

"Hey, don't worry about anything," Colleen said sympathetically. "You'll have a great time, honest. These Cotillions are so cool."

I smiled nervously at her and rubbed my palms down my pant legs.

"Wish Dad was here to see how grown-up you look," she said nicely. I smiled again.

"Thanks."

She pulled up in front of the auditorium. "I'll be back at eleven. Be sure and be right here."

"I will," I said distractedly as I watched other students walking up the broad steps to the auditorium entrance. Everyone was dressed to the nines.

"Have a good time," Colleen said with a hopeful smile. "Remember the box step."

"I will," I replied, flashing a brief smile. "Bye." I got out of the car.

I danced exactly once that evening, and it wasn't a fast dance with the box step. It was a slow dance toward the end of the evening after I had finally, after a couple of agonizing hours, worked up the nerve to ask a girl to dance. I had watched mostly and observed that the slow dancing seemed much easier than fast dancing. But I felt like a wooden Indian as my partner and I stood moving gently from side to side, arms outstretched and our hands on each other's shoulders, as if we were trying to keep each other apart.

I observed some of the kids, mostly upperclassmen, who were good at dancing fast. I knew I wasn't ready for that. A lot of the kids, mostly underclassmen, looked like dorks when they danced fast. I wasn't about to act like that either. So I had stood along the walls along with most of the male underclassmen, talking and watching.

When the dance was over I waited outside on the front steps for my sister. I watched as some of the boys and girls who had paired up during the night held hands. Some were even making out. It was astonishing to watch. I wondered what making out was like. Although I didn't know firsthand, it nonetheless was beginning to create the predictable response. I shifted uncomfortably, wishing Colleen would arrive.

⟤⟞

The seasons passed and gorgeous north Texas springs gave way to the long, hot summers. The summers blended into fall and lawns began to brown over and the trees faded from their green glory, their leaves beginning to wither and fall as winds from the Great Plains picked up in earnest, bringing a crisp snap to the night air at Friday night football games in the town stadium. Soon, winter settled in, which had disappointed my brothers and me our first winter there with its bleakness and lack of snow. Coming from the northern climes of New Jersey, we knew the joys of sledding down a hill packed with fresh snow. North Texas winters are an unremarkable brown with piercing bitter winds. We nursed our nostalgia for sledding by carrying flattened cardboard boxes to an overpass on Farm Road 1417 and sliding down the long, dry grasses of the embankment.

Our father returned to the family from back East just before Christmas of my seventh-grade year. He left the company he had worked many years for, frustrated at how things were going. The house had not sold. He could hear the growing stress in his wife's voice over the phone as she tried to manage home, six children, and work. When he sensed a breaking point looming, he made a decision for family over career and came home where he was needed.

By the time of my father's homecoming I was feeling like a different person. Adolescence had arrived in me. Upon entering the home all my siblings had flown into our father's arms with hugs and kisses. I stood apart, watching.

"Give your father a hug," my mother encouraged, puzzled by my reserve.

"I just wanna shake hands," I replied sheepishly. I held out my hand.

"Oh, come on," she urged. She seemed concerned now about her husband's reaction to a boy who had clearly changed since my father had left the previous January. Dad stood in place a bit awkwardly, gauging me. I had changed. Not any taller, perhaps a little sturdier. But there was something more, something my father seemed to be trying to decipher. After a moment he shrugged. I was a teenager now, and he would have to adjust himself to this new threshold in one of his growing children.

"That's fine," my father said. He smiled at me, taking my extended hand and pumping it.

═══◆═══

"...you will bend and tell me that you love me..."

My mind grew away from the neighborhood, which had lost its Camelot appeal over me after Stevie Walsh and the others had snuffed my illusion of safety. I still spent lone, comforting hours in the fields and woods surrounding it, escaping in the earth's love and my own dreams. Save for the occasional slinging of names such as queer, queerbait, or any of the other usual boyhood exhortations to suck, bite, or eat someone's pecker, which always pierced me through my lonesome heart, I managed adequately enough for myself, navigating the tricky path of junior high adolescence.

I developed preferences for my favorite and least favorite subjects. PE ranked at the top, for after all, I was a boy who loved to play. This was followed by English, which fed my love for books, world geography, which fired my imagination for faraway places, and history. Especially seventh-grade history. In Texas, where pride in the state keeps it perennially poised to function very nicely, thank you, as its own sovereign nation, seventh-grade history is a state-mandated rite of indoctrination into Texas pride. Seventh-grade history spent the entire year on the great state of Texas. Texas history, Texas geography, notable Texans, of which there were many, Texas industry, Texas agriculture, and on and on. I loved it. I could name all the major rivers, major crops, and important dates in history (the whole of 1836 was my favorite, being both the year of the Alamo and Texas independence). I knew that Texas was its own country for ten years and that there were 204 counties.

Least favorite subjects were science and math. Eighth-grade science intrigued me, not so much because of the subject, but because I had a male teacher, which was still a rarity. That male teacher was also Black. Mr. Snead looked just like George Washington Carver to me. I read his biography, mistaking it for a book about George Washington in the school library. I was fascinated by the story of the very smart former slave who became an agro-scientist. Mr. Snead had a portly, gentlemanly demeanor about him. He also had strict expectations. I suffered as the periodic table never made sense and I couldn't figure out where dew came from. I eked by. Same for math, where Mr. Clarkson, my seventh-grade homeroom teacher, was also my math teacher that year. The only interesting feature about Mr. Clarkson for me and the other boys was that he had a habit of pointing at anything with his middle finger instead of his index finger. All of us boys enjoyed imitating him. I was so poor at math that I found myself at a desk in one of Mr. Clarkson's summer school classes after my eighth-grade year.

I would, however, remember eighth-grade math forever. Not for the subject matter or the teacher. Eighth-grade math class was where I fell in love for the first time in my life, at first sight.

I was sitting at my desk daydreaming as usual as Mrs. Martin droned on at the blackboard. The classroom door opened and in walked Susan Whisman. She was tall and willowy, with long blond hair, blue eyes, and freckles. My chin dropped to my chest. I watched, mesmerized by her beauty as Mrs. Martin walked over and took a piece of paper from her hand that explained her new student status, and then turned and introduced her to the class.

"Boys and girls," she said in a soft voice, "this is Susan, and she's a new student to the school. Welcome, Susan," Mrs. Martin smiled sweetly at her.

This beautiful creature that suddenly had me alert and attentive made a dismissive roll of her eyes, trying to mask her own discomfort in a new environment with an air of cool aloofness. It worked spectacularly for me.

Mrs. Martin looked around the classroom and picked out a desk. "Right this way, Susan," she said leading the way.

To my utter amazement, Mrs. Martin selected a desk right beside my own. Susan plopped her three-ring binder and books on top of the desk and folded herself into the seat. My mouth was still agape. She had on a perfume that intoxicated me. She would be the reason I sat in Mr. Clarkson's summer school math class after the school year.

I could not take my eyes off her. Mrs. Martin made her way back to the front of the class and continued with the lesson. She could have been shouting "Fire!" for all I knew.

She was beautiful to me. I didn't know why, she just was. She had a subtle sadness about her that I connected with, which only made her more beautiful. She tossed her hair back, and I thought, if the teacher calls on me right now I'm dead. I shifted in my seat to accommodate the usual, involuntary physiological response. I was almost dizzy.

It took me a week to work up the nerve to say anything to her. Mrs. Martin's class was the only one we shared. Where once I dreaded the class, now I was early every day. I would see her sometimes in the hallways between periods, occasionally following her to see where she went for class. She had the air of a hippie, strolling nonchalantly through the halls talking easily with anyone regardless of race, rich or poor, band geek or jock. She wore beads and bracelets and short skirts that purpled the mysteries of my puberty.

Then, in math class one day, I noticed that what I first took for hippie decorations in the plastic lining of her binder were actually newspaper clippings. When she left her seat once and asked to go to the girl's room, I looked over at her desk and peered closer at them.

"LOCAL MARINE KILLED IN VIETNAM," one of the headlines read. I swallowed hard. I was very familiar with the news from Vietnam. I looked at another. "LOCAL MARINE GUNNER'S HELICOPTER SHOT DOWN OVER SOUTH VIETNAM."

I was still looking at the clippings, reading the articles when Susan came back through the door. I jerked my head forward, hoping she hadn't noticed. I didn't want her thinking I was nosy.

After class I followed her in the hallway. I was dying to say something, anything. I wanted her to know I existed. My palms were sweaty.

"I'm sorry 'bout your dad," I said, my voice cracking. She didn't turn around. I kept following, clearing my throat.

"Sorry 'bout your dad," I said loudly enough to make me wince.

She turned around and looked at me. Her expression was unreadable. "Excuse me?"

"Um, I said sorry 'bout your dad. Saw it on your binder."

She glanced down at the binder in her arms. "Thanks," she said with a brief smile. She turned and walked away. I stood there watching. She had actually said something to me. I turned it over in my mind. She actually looked straight at me and said something. In fact, she had said thanks. She didn't ignore me. She didn't call me a queerbait. She said thanks. I stood there watching her disappear down the hallway more in love than ever.

This first love was a salvation, a refuge from a lonely existence in the midst of a crowded humanity at school and home. It made me feel normal, like a part of everything going on around me, especially at school. I was doing what the others were doing, walking a girl to class, talking sweet nothings, and writing her name on my book covers. We wrote notes to each other that I kept and read over and over.

She seemed bemused at first by my earnestness, but I think it touched her as well. In her own dark world of secrets, tragedy, and loss, I was as unpretentious and accepting as anyone she had known. There was absolutely nothing she could mistrust or fear in me. My heart was on my sleeve, and I followed her like a puppy. I would've gladly marched into hell with a snowball upon her request. Such open devotion won her over.

For me, she was the kindest person I knew. She never laughed at me or made fun. She paid attention to me when I spoke to her. She made me feel special in a way I never had felt before. It was an introduction to love that was a gift, manna from the heavens for a boy with a sad heart who was too small for football and wondered where I fit in. I would love her the rest of my life for that.

WHEN WORLDS COLLIDE

"...And I shall hear, tho' soft you tread above me
And all my grave will warmer, sweeter be..."

It's a curious thing, the world of boys. In adulthood, we are often amazed to find that our memories of boyhood are often at odds with the collective memories of family, friends, or history. Men often carry memories of events that either never occurred, occurred to someone else or in another decade from when we remember, or in a sequence at total odds from everyone else's recollections. We stubbornly cling to our own recall. The curious world of boys simply becomes the curious world of men.

Such was my boyhood. I operated within the constellation of my family, extended family, and friends, yet was frequently aloft in my own orbit. My world was only what I cared to pay attention to.

In my early years growing up in a small, northern New Jersey town a mere fifteen miles from the thrumming pulse of New York City, I couldn't recall ever seeing a person of color. All logic said that I certainly had. Although the small town I lived in was almost totally White, my family made frequent trips into New York City during the years we lived there. I'd been to the Museum of Natural History, but Martians could have been walking around the place for all I knew. I cared only and passionately for the dinosaur exhibit. My mother had taken my brothers and me to Macy's during the holidays to sit on Santa's lap. There could have been a hundred Frankensteins and Draculas lurking around, and I never would have known. All I cared about was giving Santa my list. Such was my singular focus upon those things I cared for that I noticed little else around me.

There was nothing my parents had done or said to form any impression of others different from me. Despite their Great Depression-era upbringing and the long, hard, and uncertain years of the war that shaped a pragmatic, conservative outlook about life, they were, nonetheless, warm and kind people. Some of the fondest memories I had, substantiated by the rest of my siblings, were ones of open displays of affection. Hugs were common. Every child was kissed good night. Our father openly adored our mother and doted kindly on her. None of us had ever heard a word of anger from our father toward our mother. He treated her with gentle deference. He was a born romantic, frequently given to spontaneous episodes of sudden hugs and deep, bend-over kisses on the cheek. Mother was a bit more reserved and acerbic with her tongue, but we could see she loved her husband's affection and adored him in return.

I had no memory of unkind words about other people or cultures from my parents. There was no racist talk or scornful judgments of others. My parents lived the "live and let live" credo. Comments about individuals, however, were a bit different. From my years in New Jersey in the early sixties I heard my parents talking warily of Adam Clayton Powell, Martin Luther King, and Sammy Davis Jr. My parents were wary of a lot of things then, like the communist menace, Soviet nuclear missiles, hippies, and rock-n-roll. The family sat around the TV one night in 1964 and watched the Beatles on *The Ed Sullivan Show*. I was eight. Mother told us how the Beatles wore curlers at night because their hair was so long and they were probably criminally dangerous, owing to the stylish, pointy shoes they wore.

Surely I had encountered people of other races. It was not my memory though until, that is, I sat down at my desk on the opening day of fourth grade in my new hometown in north Texas.

My neighborhood school was on the west side of this long-segregated town, situated in a corner of an expansive bucolic park. The park was dotted with shady groves and athletic fields. At one end was the municipal pool. It was surrounded by neat, middle-class brick ranch-style homes peopled by nice, White folk. So it was a shock of a most natural kind when I looked to my side to see who my neighbor was at the next desk over and laid my eyes on Beverly Campbell.

She sat in her seat very self-consciously, the only Negro in the class. She wore a plain hand-me-down, but very clean dress. Her skin was a rich, deep chocolate. Her jet-black hair was smooth and neatly combed to the nape of her neck. Her eyes were the deepest brown I had ever seen and, well, I could not keep my eyes off her. She was the most curious creature I'd ever seen.

She furtively returned my look. I continued to stare at this most exotic young girl. She glanced again at me, only to see me continuing to stare. Mrs. Bankston was in front of the class talking. I didn't hear her. I only wanted to try to figure out how on earth there could be such a person of such a color. I couldn't take my eyes away.

She looked away, then back again. The skinny little kid next to her was beginning to annoy her, even if he was White. I saw the look of annoyance, noticing the flare of her nostrils. It didn't register; such was the state of my curiosity. She turned her head more sharply toward me now, barely whispering something I couldn't hear. I continued to examine her, oblivious to anything else, including Mrs. Bankston.

Suddenly, with a lightning flick of her hand, she reached out and smacked me lightly right on the nose. My head snapped back, suddenly angry I had been hit by a girl. She immediately looked fearful, something I didn't understand. I thought, *Did she think I was gonna hit her back or somethin'?* Every boy knew that as soon as you hit a girl, it was all over. Even if it wasn't your fault. A boy always got in trouble. Boys weren't supposed to hit girls. I looked around to see if anyone was watching, especially another boy. I wanted to get off on the right foot with the new boys in my class and show them how fast I could run and how good I was at football during recess. I didn't want them thinking I was some kind of sissy 'cause I'd been hit by a girl. Thankfully, the whole episode went unnoticed.

I regarded Beverly Campbell warily after that. Secretly, I was amazed at how fast she could run. She was faster than all but a few of the boys. I was usually locked in a grim neck and neck race with her whenever we happened to be close to one another. It was like racing my shadow. She was a superior kick ball player, and the girls loved having her on their team. I also noticed that she routinely had better grades on her papers than I did, especially in math. I developed a grudging respect for her.

The following year I moved to another, west side school for fifth and sixth grade. The only Negro there was the janitor.

═══◈══

My experiences at Friday night football games at the town stadium gave me another glimpse into the world of Negroes I was now accustomed to seeing in town, though I never had occasion to speak to one. The gridiron was the one place in Texas where boys of any race had an opportunity to be together in safety. If you were big and strong and fast, color didn't matter. Only the game did. But wandering the stands during the games, I could hear the way the athletes were discussed by tobacco-chewing men in cowboy hats and overalls, upper-class high school kids whose parents bought cars for them, ladies groups in attendance, and even clergymen sitting in the stands.

Negroes in the stands were scarce, as not a lot of their sons played on the town high school team. Most were over at Fred Douglass High.

I would walk through the stands and bleachers, listening to snatches of conversation from people gathered in their groups as I passed.

"That McKnight kid," one would say, "helluva quarterback. Ain't his daddy with the Kiwanas? Nice family. Kid's got an arm, don't he?"

"Lookit the way that nigger can run! What's that boy's name, anyway? All them can run like greased lightnin'. Shit, you can see the whites of their eyes from here!" Raucous laughter.

Or, "Jesus, look at all them spics they got on their team. Glad I don't live in Dallas!"

I was oblivious to such distinctions. The rigid, invisible lines separating folks according to color was unknown to me. I would watch the football players, mesmerized. It didn't matter to me what color they were on the field, White, Black, or if they were Mexican or Indian. They played their hearts out, and, when the home team scored a touchdown, it didn't matter what color the scorer was. The crowd went wild, and all one would ever read about the next day in the paper was victory. At the end of a game I would stand at the gate at the end of the field where all the players walked off, watching the dirty, bloody, and exhausted warriors. I saw teammates talking, smiling, and jostling each other. I did not see White, Black, or Mexican. I was unaware of such differences. It thrilled me to watch them go by.

⟺

Junior high life and its attendant cultural requirements and the diligence that must be paid by all of its young inhabitants to prevent humiliating disasters and navigate its seas of uncertainty became my preeminent concern. Its demands pulled me from the neighborhood, segregated by its geographical remoteness at the edge of town. I seldom ventured further than a few houses away from my own anymore.

My golden Schwinn Stingray leaned unused against a wall in the garage. I discharged myself from active duty in the neighborhood war games and their running battles through the yards, the alley, and the nearby woods. The trampoline lost its gravitational pull on me. The Swiss Family Robinson tree maintained a patient vigil.

I still took to the pastures and woods, usually alone, as was my preference. Sometimes I would take my .410 shotgun, which I received that Christmas during my seventh-grade year. My failure to produce a merit badge after camp only intensified my lobbying efforts. Receiving the shotgun had finally bought my parents some peace. My father was strict about its use, allowing me to use it only when he was accompanying me, even though my father refused to carry a gun. But I would still take it with me often when I went off alone into the woods. I got the occasional rabbit or quail. The quail I would clean in the field and leave for foxes. The rabbits I took home and skinned.

I needed thinking time these days. The beloved land gave me that. It still loved my bare feet upon her ancient, soft skin. She gave me space in my mind now as I pondered the vicissitudes of early teenage life, just as she had given space for my physical needs for freedom of movement. Most of all, she gave me peace and comfort.

A dizzying array of new characters inhabited my world now at school that literally crowded out the companions I had in my neighborhood for the past few years. Of primary importance to me were my fellow teammates on the football, basketball, and track teams. The world of athletics stripped away cultural, racial, and socioeconomic status from all its participants; White, Black, Indian, and Hispanic. Good ol' boy coaches, many of them White men from the ranches of the wide, rural county lands surrounding the town admired, mentored, and developed the Black and Hispanic players with talent as equally as any other player. Discrimination from the coaches came in the form of the athletic talent levels of the players. Texas football centered on winning traditions. If you were good, you played. If you weren't, you didn't.

The Black athletes, many of whom had seldom had so much contact or shared such close quarters with White kids, seemed to delight in expanding the horizons of cool for their White counterparts. Soon, every team member was performing handshakes in the "soul grasp" from young Black culture, even if it was White on White.

On long bus rides to distant towns for games, I sat in my seat enormously entertained by the boisterous back and forth between the Black kids as they laughed and talked about each other and their world of which I knew nothing. They played in bands in church and sang in the choir, sang Marvin Gaye and Aaron Neville songs with unbridled enthusiasm in the bus, and talked about sex. Their ribald descriptions of their sexual exploits enthralled me. They seemed so worldly and hip. They seemed to know more about girls than I could ever imagine.

I also sensed, but did not understand, a restless anger flowing under the outward behavior of the Black kids I knew on the team and saw in the hallways and classrooms at school. I was unaware of the deep chasm separating the folks in town by race. They seemed always ready for a challenge from anyone at anytime. Sometimes, I would hear some of the White kids whispering among themselves, saying "yeah, they're fine one on one with ya, but get a few of them together and then they're trouble." I was puzzled by it. I noticed it most whenever the subject of rights or social justice or Black power came up on the blacktop playground, the cafeteria, a team bus ride, or in the hallways. Black fists would rise up together among a group of Black kids in the hallways, as raised voices would shout, "MLK, MLK!" as this young, fearless generation of Black youth looked at the world their parents and grandparents had eked by in and began to push back and fill that chasm bit by bit with a youthful courage that didn't know where the traps and dangers lay. If they did, they didn't care. They had no patience for the world as it was, as it had always been for them. It was their world now.

I have learned over the long years that the collective memory of an enslaved, yet undefeated and enduring people runs deeper in the soul than the memory of the dominant, privileged, and afflu-ent whose history and stories of desperation, fear, and survival have faded, relegated to pages in history books, genealogies, and family lore. The privileged and the powerful refer to their ancestors' plights with quaint, misplaced pride. Their claims of connection to ancestral struggles have been diluted by the enduring dominance of their sta-tion in society.

Not so with the Negro in my north Texas grain mill town. Black kids in my junior high were indelibly stamped with the painful history of their people in this sleepy, insular place. All of them knew, listen-ing to their parents and grandparents, how dangerous life could be owing to the color of their skin. All of them knew the name of George Hughes very well.

According to those who knew George, which by 1968 was every Black adult over forty years of age in town, George was known for being a little crazy. No one quite knew what drove George to do what he did. Perhaps he had just had enough of the White man's world and the White man's rules.

George showed up at a farm outside of town one day at the be-ginning of May 1930, angry and desperate. The farm owner, a White man, owed George back wages. The farmer's missus told George her husband was in town. George left, but somewhere along the line he decided enough was enough. That farmer had put him off too long. He showed up back at the farm a little later with a shotgun. In the middle of a heated argument between George and the farmer's wife, both of them scared to death about what was happening, George assaulted the poor woman and beat her. Several people around the house heard the commotion and raced to her aid. George fired off a few rounds in the air with his shotgun, hitting no one. He ran off, being chased by the White folks who were so enraged they pursued him unarmed.

A deputy sheriff later arrested George and took him to the county courthouse, which occupied the town square. After a couple of days George was charged with criminal assault and the trial was set to commence four days later. The judge pledged a quick trial. The Constitution may guarantee a speedy trial, but every Negro in town knew what the judge meant by "speedy trial." The trial never happened.

In the days before the trial, rumors spread like wildfire through town that George had mutilated and raped the poor woman. Medical examination of both George and the woman proved otherwise, but that did nothing to calm the growing fury. Officers removed George from the jail and hid him away, and even gave tours of the jail to disbelieving townsfolk to show he wasn't there, hoping to defuse the situation. It did not. A growing, menacing crowd of thousands gathered nightly outside the courthouse.

On the day of the trial, three Texas Rangers and a local police sergeant brought George to the courthouse. The sheriff and his deputies lined the courtroom and corridors as an all-White jury was selected. An angry crowd of five thousand people from all over the region gathered on the town square. Those who could made their way inside. Someone paraded around outside the courthouse with an American flag, whipping the crowd into an angry mood.

The jury was sworn in at noon, the charges were read to George, and, perhaps because he'd simply had enough of everything, enough of every insult, every degradation, every wrong damn thing he'd ever seen or been subjected to his whole life, he pleaded guilty.

The crowds in the town square then forced the doors of the courtroom. A couple of the Rangers fired warning shots into the air. It didn't work. Shortly after, tear gas was set off in the building. George was taken downstairs to the court vault for safekeeping. The fire department responded to the scene and placed ladders to the windows to allow women and children to escape the gas.

The judge, having escaped the tear gas, dithered in his office, trying to decide if he should order a change of venue. After a couple of wasted hours, the mob decided for him.

An open can of gasoline was thrown through the tax collector's window, starting a fire. The fire quickly spread throughout the building. Officials escaped through the windows, aided once again by ladders thrown by the fire department.

Deputies said afterward they offered to escort George Hughes from the vault to the county jail for safety, but that he refused, choosing, instead, to stay locked in the vault. From that moment to the present time, not a single Black person in town ever believed the deputies. They believed otherwise, that in the choking heat of the fire, the deputies fled for their safety, leaving poor George to cook alive inside the locked vault.

Outside, the mob cut the fire hoses and otherwise thwarted the fire department's efforts to quell the blaze. By four o'clock in the afternoon, all that remained of the building were the exterior walls and the indestructible vault.

By 6:30 that evening, the crazed mob was locked in a pitched battle with National Guardsmen sent by Governor Moody. Emboldened by the belief the Guardsmen would not fire upon a crowd of White people, they drove the militia out of town. With hearts black with ignorant rage and hands as strong as the devil, they went to work like soulless goblins on the vault. By midnight, using hammers and acetylene torches, they cut the vault open and pulled George Hughes's body out and threw it into the street. The crowd of people whooped, yelled, and cheered as George's body was tied to the back of a truck and dragged around the streets of downtown and into the Negro section. There, in front of a Black-owned drugstore, his body was lynched in a nearby tree. Men from the mob broke into the drugstore and dragged furniture out and placed it under George's body. Setting fire to the pile, they incinerated his corpse.

The mob then set fire to the drugstore and several other Black-owned businesses and blockaded the streets to prevent the fire department from extinguishing the conflagration. By morning of the next day, most of the town's Negro business section, as well as a few houses, lay in ashes.

George's body was cut down by deputies and offered to two black-owned funeral homes. But the parlors were among the buildings burned to the ground and so had no facilities to take the body. George was taken to a White-owned funeral home, then out to the county farm and buried without ceremony.

Of the thousands of White folks who gathered as a mob, burned down the courthouse killing George Hughes, and drove off the Guardsmen and deputies and set fire to the Negro business section, only fourteen were indicted on any charges. By October of 1931, only two of those men charged were convicted, one for rioting and one for arson. Both received only two-year sentences.

The local newspaper lamented the lawlessness, property damage, and notoriety brought upon the town. It was not lost on the Black folks that not a single note of regret over the murder of George Hughes was expressed in the paper. No one held their breath waiting for such an expression either.

The memory seared deep into the collective consciousness of the Negro community. And every one of my Black classmates knew the story as if it had happened only last year. What was changing, however, was the sense of fear that had run like an undercurrent through the Negro section of town since George Hughes's murder. A youthful anger was emerging, challenging the uneasy status quo.

I had heard snatches of the story from time to time, whispered among the boys in my neighborhood. I never gave it much thought, thinking the story a relic from the faded past, like World War I, or the invention of the light bulb. I was clueless to the dark current of racism flowing under the sun-drenched, serene-looking town.

"Do you know what we up against?" Randy Cross, one of the Black kids on the football team, said to me one day as we stood waiting our turn in a four square line after lunch.

"No, what?" I answered, bewildered.

"White people!" Randy replied.

"How come?"

Randy looked at me like I was a bug or something. "Man, where you been? On Mars?" He shook his head in exasperation. "Jus' remember, little man, we Black. An' we together. Black is beautiful! Ya hear me?"

"Yeah, I hear ya," I replied. I attempted a Black accent. "It's cool, bro. It's cool." I smiled up at Randy, trying hard to actually be cool.

Randy shook his head, a tiny smile playing at the corners of his mouth. "You're a trip, little dude." He turned away and took his turn at the game, stepping into a square.

⊏⟨⟩⊐

I developed a friendship in seventh grade with DeMarcus Rayford, another Black kid on the football team. We shared a very important common bond. We were both fourth-stringers. We often knelt together on the sidelines during practice, nursing our scrapes and bruises as the first- and second-stringers scrimmaged. Being largely ignored at this point during practice, the fourth-stringers were left to our own devices and pretty much entertained ourselves till the coach blew his whistle for everyone to line up for the wind sprints at the end of practice.

DeMarcus was shy with me, knowing much more than I did about the gulf between our worlds. I only knew our lot was cast together as fourth-stringers. DeMarcus had an older sister in the ninth grade who I had seen in the hallways. She was beautiful and exotic looking and had a radiant smile. There was always a crowd of boys around her.

"Your sister sure is popular," I said one day as we knelt side by side on the edge of the playing field, examining our bruises.

"They's always boys where I stay," DeMarcus said, rolling his eyes and raising his eyebrows in exasperation.

"Yeah, same here," I replied. "I got two sisters with guys always callin' an' comin' over."

I looked at DeMarcus. "You got a girlfriend?"

DeMarcus smiled. "Naw. Ain't got one yet."

"Me neither. I danced with a girl at the Cotillion dance, though."

"Yeah? Who?"

"Valerie from geography class. How come you didn't go?"

DeMarcus shrugged and looked out on the field. "Lookit O'Quinn Polk there makin' that tackle!" he said, changing the subject.

I looked out on the field at O'Quinn, a small, compact Black kid with a loud voice who enjoyed being the center of attention. We could hear him on the field.

"Pow! Take that, man!" O'Quinn shouted as he got up from the ground and stood over the fallen ball carrier.

"That boy get pussy anytime he feel like it," DeMarcus said, looking at O'Quinn enviously. "Girls jus' can't say no!"

I looked at O'Quinn. Already he seemed more like a man to me. Then I turned to DeMarcus. "Hey," I said impulsively, "ya wanna come spend the night at my house Saturday night?"

"What?" DeMarcus looked at me with an incredulous expression on his face.

"Spend the night," I said hopefully. I was extending myself here. Being assertive wasn't my strong suit. I pressed on. "This Saturday. Ya wanna?"

"I dunno," DeMarcus replied doubtfully. Never in his life had he slept in a White person's house. He had seldom ever been in a White person's house.

"It'd be fun!" I continued enthusiastically. "We could sleep in our guest bedroom so my brothers couldn't bug us. It's got a TV in it an' my dad's gone right now so we could watch till sign off time if we want long as we keep the sound down."

DeMarcus looked at me. "Yore daddy gone too?"

"Yeah," I replied.

"You know where he at?"

"A course. He's in New Jersey. Where's your dad?"

DeMarcus looked away toward the field and said nothing. I pressed on for the sleepover.

"An' we can play football in the backyard. An' I got an electric football game!"

The electric football game was a strong incentive for DeMarcus. No one he knew had one. He assumed they were for rich folk. He'd seen them on television commercials, though, and they seemed like a lot of fun. The game was a rectangular-shaped thin metal tray about thirty inches long and twenty inches wide. Small plastic-molded football players, about an inch and a half tall, were placed in offensive and defensive positions on the playing surface that was painted to look like a football field. When all the players were set, an electric switch was turned on, causing the entire playing surface to start vibrating with a loud humming noise and causing the figures to start moving on the surface. Some just rotated uselessly around in circles. Some of them jammed up all together in a scrum that went nowhere. Sometimes, though, if the figures were set up just right, an actual play would develop. Occasionally, the ball carrier, who carried a small piece of fabric cut into the shape of a football tucked under a rigid arm by one of the game's players, would spring loose into the open field. If it was pointed in the right direction and didn't suddenly veer off toward the sideline and out of bounds, as would often happen, it would vibrate along the surface all the way down and score a touchdown. My brothers and I had hours of fun with it.

DeMarcus looked at me. "Really? You got one of them?"

"Yup," I replied, sensing I had set the hook. "We can play it as much as we want. It's got all the players too. You can even be the Dallas Cowboys if you want."

DeMarcus nodded to himself and looked out on the field. It sounded like fun.

"You got your own bedroom?" he asked.

"Naw. Me an' my brothers gotta share."

DeMarcus knew what sharing space was like. "Okay. I'll ask my ma."

"Cool!" I exclaimed.

Coach blew his whistle. "Everybody, let's go! On the goal line!" He spat a long line of tobacco juice. "Hustle up, boys! C'mon, my supper's waitin'!"

⟫⟪

I believe God knows well how the children of creation can entertain and delight. It's one of the reasons why they exist. When a good laugh is needed to counter the awful cruelties inflicted by folks upon one another, God turns to the little ones. By virtue of their innocence, sacred laughter rings mellifluously through the heavens.

And so it was that two twelve-year-old boys, separated by deep, rigid boundaries over three hundred years in the making in the New World, stood together in the downstairs bathroom of my home looking at ourselves in the mirror as we prepared for bed that Saturday night.

It had been a grand time. It took a couple of puzzling days for my mother to try to figure out what her son was about, but in the end saw my request for what it was. I wanted a simple sleepover with a friend. It was something I hadn't asked for in a long time. During the summer it had been virtually a daily request, either for a friend at our home or me at another house, usually Billy Swift's. Those requests had died off suddenly a few weeks before school started. She noticed from time to time my reserve and caution. I kept to myself more.

So, when I had come home and excitedly asked for a sleepover with a friend from the football team, she was pleased and said it was fine, so long as she talked to the other boy's parents first. I was ahead of her, pulling a piece of paper out of my pocket with the Rayford's phone number on it.

She called that evening and was immediately puzzled by the woman's voice on the other end. Then it came to her. The Rayfords must be one of the wealthier families in town. They even had a maid! She was impressed.

"Yes," she said, giving her name, "I would like to speak with Mrs. Rayford, please. Would you mind getting her for me?"

"Yore speakin' to her."

Silence from the other end of the phone. Mrs. Rayford waited.

"Excuse me?"

"I said, yore speakin' to her. This is Mizz Rayford."

Silence again. Then, "I, I see. Well, uhh, er, I'm calling because my son has asked if your son can spend the night Saturday at our home."

"Thas' what my boy tol' me too!" Mrs. Rayford said. "Tell th' truth, it kinda s'prised me. But he seems 'cited to go!"

"Well, my son is excited as well. I wanted to call to introduce myself and make arrangements to pick your son up."

"Thas' mighty nice, ma'am," Mrs. Rayford said jovially. She sensed she had the upper hand on this one. DeMarcus had come home talking about the White kid that was his friend now and everything seemed okay about it. DeMarcus had fairly begged her for permission to spend the night. Like most parents of adolescents, she spent a lot of time trying to figure her kids out. She had experienced precious few positive interactions with White folks in her lifetime. There had certainly been some ugly ones. This lady she had on the phone seemed nice enough, though she obviously hadn't been fully informed of the situation. The thought of that White woman's expression right now made her smile.

"Umm, yes, well," my mother continued, "if it's all right with you, we can pick your son up Saturday morning, and then bring him back Sunday morning before church."

"Thas' kind of you," said Mrs. Rayford. "But no need to bother yorself bringin' 'im back. We's goin' to Whitesboro Sunday mornin' so we be headed out Route 82 by yore place. We can pick 'im up early if thas' alright."

"Yes. Yes, I suppose it is," she had replied distractedly. She took down their address and hung up. Then she looked at me bemusedly.

"You didn't tell me he was a Negro."

"It's Black, Mom," I corrected. "That's what the Black kids on my team tol' me."

"Well, Black, then," she said. "You didn't say he was Black."

I merely shrugged. "Are we gonna go get 'im?"

"Uh-huh," she nodded. "I have to find out where his street is, though. I haven't even heard of it."

"He lives over by the Quaker Oats mill!"

So DeMarcus Rayford came over Saturday morning for an overnight. My brothers regarded him as a supreme novelty. They fawned over him, watching every move he made. They let him have the first turn at everything we did out in the backyard. They fell over themselves trying to be the one next to him all the time, or helping him with anything, or getting anything DeMarcus needed. They asked if they could touch his hair, embarrassing me to no end. DeMarcus seemed to take everything in stride, though he was as self-conscious as a boy could be. He was impeccably polite.

In the afternoon we watched the summer Olympics in Mexico City on TV. DeMarcus was enthralled by color TV. All of us kept careful track of the medal count, cheering as the USA was leading the way. The announcers kept talking about Tommy Smith and John Carlos.

Willie turned to DeMarcus. "Didja see they kicked out those two USA guys for giving the Black power sign?"

DeMarcus looked at him without saying anything. He gave his shoulder a slight shrug.

"They shouldn' have done it," Willie continued. "My ma says you're supposed to back your country, right or wrong."

DeMarcus remained silent.

"Do ya think they shoulda done it?" Willie pressed.

My brothers and I all looked at DeMarcus. He shifted uncomfortably in his seat. Again, he gave a small shrug.

I sensed DeMarcus's discomfort.

"Shut up, twerp," I said, low and menacing. "C'mon, DeMarcus, let's go outside."

Once we were outside I looked at him. "Don't pay any attention to them," I said. "They're just in elementary school."

"Do you think Carlos and Smith were wrong?" DeMarcus looked at me evenly.

I shrugged. "Who cares? They won the 200, right? They can do whatever they want. It's a free country." I picked up a football and gave it a punt across the yard.

DeMarcus regarded me with a thoughtful expression. He gazed down at the ground for a moment, then spit. Looking up, he eyed the dam bordering the backyard.

"Ya got catfish in there?"

After supper, we climbed up into my tree fort platform. We played football in the yard till it was dark. We watched *Combat* on TV in the den. DeMarcus and I then went to the guest room to watch our own TV and play the electric football game. I had a hard time getting rid of my brothers.

"Ma!" I shouted, out of patience. "Will you tell these buttholes to leave us alone?"

"Speak in a nicer tone, will you?" my mother said crossly as she herded the other three boys out of the guest room and up to their own room.

Later that evening, she knocked on the guest room door and opened it up. "It's late boys. Time for bed."

"Aww," I lamented.

"Time for bed," she intoned with finality. She left, closing the door.

We turned off the football game. "I'll show ya how to run the game with no 'lectricity," I whispered conspiratorially. "It's quieter so we can keep playin'."

"How?"

"Ya just tap your finger on it quickly an' lightly like this," I said. I demonstrated by taking my index finger and tapping softly and rapidly in the corner of the game's metal surface. DeMarcus watched as it made all the figures move just like when the electricity was on. And it was a lot quieter.

"Thas' cool, man."

We made our way into the downstairs bathroom and closed the door. The time for some serious talk was at hand. After all, we were almost teenagers.

"What do you do at night for your pimples?" I asked as I bent closer to the mirror, scrutinizing my face.

"I use this," DeMarcus said, rummaging in his bag. He pulled out a small jar of Noxzema.

"Hey, so do I!" I took a similar dark blue jar from the cabinet below the sink and held it up.

DeMarcus nodded and looked at his reflection. "I always get pimples right here," he said, rubbing a finger across his forehead.

"I get 'em right here," I said, rubbing my fingers on both sides of my nose. "Girls don't like 'em on boys."

"I know. Seems as soon as I get rid of a couple, a couple more pop up."

"Yeah, me too. Hey, have ya seen all the pimples on Sydney in PE? He's even got 'em on his back!"

"Eeeww," DeMarcus said scrunching his face. "I know!"

We began applying the Noxzema over our faces as we talked.

"I think Debbie Monroe is cute," said I nonchalantly, looking in the mirror. "I might ask her to go steady." I continued applying the smooth white cream.

"Yeah? I kinda like Velma Thurston." DeMarcus finished applying the cream and stood back, looking at his reflection in the mirror.

I looked at myself as well. We glanced at each other's reflections and started to giggle.

"You look like you jus' saw Casper the Ghost," I said, beginning to laugh harder.

"You look like someone just threw a pie in yore face!" DeMarcus replied laughing as well.

"Girls like a smooth face."

"Sho' do," DeMarcus said.

DeMarcus looked back in the mirror, leaning across the sink. He began humming to himself. After a moment, I recognized the tune.

"I know that one," I said. "It's cool."

Both of us began softly singing the lyrics.

"Give me a ticket for an airplane… Ain't got time for a fast train! Lonely days are gone! I'm a goin' home! My baby she wrote me a letter!"

I picked up a hairbrush and held it like a microphone. DeMarcus struck a pose as if he were a backup singer from one of the Motown groups. We lit into the refrain of the Box Tops' classic.

"Well, she wrote me a letter! Said she couldn't live without me no more! Mister, can't ya see I jus' gotta get back to my baby once more… anywayyyy!"

We ended the refrain with gusto and broke out laughing. From upstairs we heard my mother's voice. She had the tone of muted annoyance that I understood well.

"Boys…"

"Okay, Ma," I called back, mustering the right tone of contriteness.

We looked at each other with our white Noxzema faces and burst into a fit of giggling we tried hard to suppress. I farted loudly, sending us into renewed peals of laughter.

"Boys!" Sharper this time. I knew we'd reached our limit.

"Sorry," I called hoping to sound even more contrite.

"To bed!"

"Okay...."

We managed to compose ourselves. We waited a few minutes while the Noxzema worked its magic before washing it off, then toweled our faces and got into our beds. I decided discretion was the better part of valor and so suggested resuming the electric football game in the morning, to which DeMarcus was agreeable. I was excited to be sleeping in a different room than my brothers for a change. The air was better down here, I thought. I felt happy having a friend for a sleepover.

We talked softly about girls, who the meanest teacher in school was, and whether we would always be fourth-stringers. For a small while, the universe turned as it was meant to. Two boys, from different worlds, talking about things that adolescent schoolboys everywhere talk about: sports, school, and girls.

God watched us, islands of innocence in an inhumane world. God laughed, loving us two all the more for our innocent souls.

⟞⬦⟝

I was fifteen now, and the ninth grade brought many changes for both my town and me. The country's societal upheavals were beginning at long last to wash up onto the shores of the town's cloistered Southern Jim Crow society, protected all the long years from the outside world by the bosom of pastures, ranches, and farms that surrounded it. A new high school was built that would fully integrate all the town's high school students. Negro parents and White ranchers, bank managers and janitors, ladies' garden club members and their maids watched warily from their kitchens as their children went off to school and sat together in classrooms, many for the first time in their lives. Frederick Douglass High School became an elementary school, and the students at Piner moved into the former town high school, next to the shrine of the football stadium where I worshipped more fervently than any time I ever spent in church. Dillingham remained untouched.

Stephanie Sheffield moved back into town at the beginning of ninth grade. She had moved with her family halfway through seventh grade to California. Now she was back, and oh, how she had changed; all California hip now. She had long, careless blond hair that she put flowers in. She wore beads and jangly bracelets and miniskirts with high, white go-go boots. She shuffled through the hallways with a dreamy grin on her face, carrying her books and giving everyone the peace sign as she passed.

What got everyone talking about her, though, was the fact at lunchtime in the cafeteria she would deliberately sit at the table with all the Black kids. She stuck out like a candle on a dark night, sitting there quietly at the end of the table each day with her blond hair and beads as the Black kids talked quietly among themselves and cast furtive, puzzled looks her way. None of them spoke to her. After a while, a lot of White kids weren't speaking to her either. She seemed unfazed, however, and continued her odd, quixotic way of hers, wearing an easy smile all the time.

Linda Jenkins arrived for the ninth grade that year at Piner, moving into town from faraway. She was an Air Force brat and had lived in faraway exotic places like Germany and Florida. Her dad was now stationed at the air base about twenty miles outside of town. She was disarmingly pretty, poised, and confident. Her self-possessed demeanor and worldly air gained her instant access to the highest circles of junior high society. She was handily elected to the cheerleading squad by the student body during the tryout assembly in the auditorium. Linda Jenkins was also Black. And she was the first Black cheerleader anyone ever knew of, which mattered not to me. She was pretty, and she was a cheerleader. That was all I cared about.

Walking through an empty hallway one day after obtaining a hall pass under false pretenses, I spotted Linda in her cheerleading uniform loitering in a doorway, talking with several of her friends. She looked over at the shirt and tie I was wearing and recognized the required dress for all the football players on game day.

"Hi," she said, flashing her incredible smile.

"Hey, Linda," I replied, smiling shyly her way. She would always be one of those out-of-reach girls I daydreamed about.

I was passing close by and so walked up to her, ignoring the others standing around. "Ya ready for the game this afternoon?" I said, seizing any excuse to have a conversation with a pretty girl.

"Yeah, of course," she replied. "You going to get a chance to play today?"

Embarrassed, I said, "Sure."

"Good," she said.

"Hey," I said, hoping to keep the conversation going "Ya going to the Cotillion dance Saturday night? I didn't see ya at the first one."

Truth be told, I wouldn't have noticed much of anything or anyone at the first dance of the year at the end of September. That dance had been the zenith of my love affair with Susan Whisman. It was her last dance there. She told me at the beginning of the school year that she was moving with her mother to Oklahoma somewhere. The dance would be our last "date." When we slow danced together, for the first time in my life, I was glad I was short, as my head rested nicely at her breast. She always wore the same perfume, Windsong. I inhaled it as I gazed eye level at her chest. At that last dance, sitting in the shadows together along the walls of the basement hall of the Civic Auditorium, we kissed and made out as if there would be no tomorrow. In school the following Monday, Peter Bonham told me he had timed us several times on his wristwatch.

"Man," Peter said with a wolfish smile, "you guys were under for two minutes during one of those kisses!" It had made me feel quite successful and manly.

Now, I looked at Linda expectantly. I didn't think she had a boy-friend. Susan had been gone almost two months; a sufficient period of mourning had passed. Maybe, just maybe…

"Blacks aren't allowed at Cotillion," she said. There was no accusation in her voice. No recrimination. Just a statement of fact. She turned back to her entourage of girls and continued talking with them.

I stood speechless, as if I'd just been slapped across the face. How could such a simple white bread boy respond to such an impassively delivered statement of truth? A truth that had been there all along, plain as day. My mind flashed to the first week of school in each of my three years of junior high. I thought of homeroom, when those embossed Cotillion invitations were carefully handed out. I remembered not everyone received them. The realization brought me up short. No Black kids, no Hispanics, no Indians had ever received one. I had been too wrapped up in my own selfish, wounded desire for acceptance to notice the distinctions. My face flushed with shame.

I shifted on my feet, suddenly feeling very out of place. I didn't know whether to stay or go. Linda glanced over her shoulder and gave me a quick, dismissive smile. I took the signal and walked away. Suddenly I wasn't looking forward to Saturday night. The magic I had always attached to the Cotillion dances had been blown away like smoke in the wind.

In the end I went anyway. All the White football players did because it was expected. Our elevated social status as athletes bestowed certain obligations, but it felt hollow to me. I didn't dance at all, not even a slow dance. I hung out along the walls with the other boys, watching. Linda had been right. All I saw were White faces. It would be the last Cotillion dance I went to.

THE WANTING DISCIPLE

"...For you will bend and tell me...
...all the flowers are dying..."

Football! Unknown to our family, the move to Texas would take our embrace of the sport to the messianic level that is the perch of Texas high school football. Upon returning from one of his preliminary trips to Texas to pave the way for the family and settle into work, our father had raved about football in Texas and of the size of the town's high school football stadium. Upon our first game there on a warm Friday night in September, we were believers.

When I began seventh grade, I could barely contain my excitement. At long last, it was finally going to happen for me. My dream of gridiron glory was in reach. Shortly before school began a letter arrived at the house detailing a list of required things each boy would need who was interested in playing, along with a practice and game schedule. I carefully examined the schedule, memorizing it. Practice was every day after school over at the fields on Centre Street. There were eight scheduled games to be played on Thursday afternoons. Four home games, right in the town stadium. I was actually going to touch the rich green grass of that hallowed field. It was all I talked about at dinnertime. I marveled over the fact there were four away games. The team would travel on a school bus just like the high school players did to distant towns. In Texas, distance means distance. There were some away games that I wouldn't be home from until well after dark. I was thrilled.

The required equipment items were also new for me. I'd never worn a mouthpiece before. It was an initiating experience for me, this procedure of boiling a pan of water, dunking the mouthpiece in while I held the retaining strap, and then quickly and with trepidation, inserting the hot plastic piece into my mouth so I could form it with my tongue.

The most puzzling piece of equipment, though, was the jock strap. My mother looked through the display on the shelf at the drugstore while I stood apart looking embarrassed as she searched for the smallest size possible. She settled on one and tossed it in the cart along with the other items. When we arrived home, I inspected the box containing the vital protective equipment. It puzzled me. I'd never seen one before. I removed it from the box and held it up. It was a very confusing-looking apparatus. I had no idea how to don it.

On the verge of adolescence, I wasn't about to ask my mother for advice. My brothers were as puzzled as I was. Finally, I broached my dilemma to Colleen. I knew she wouldn't laugh at me. She wasn't sure how it was worn either, though if she were, she probably wouldn't have cared to supervise a lesson. But she had a solution.

"I'll get Mike over here," she said.

I brightened. Mike was not only my sister's high school steady, he was a first-string starter on the high school team. He was a Bearcat and wore number 21. Whenever he was at the house I hung close by with a goofy smile on my face and a starry look in my eyes.

When he arrived, my sister quietly explained what my need was. Mike smiled sheepishly. He shrugged, though, as if to say, "What the heck." It would earn him points with her.

He brought me upstairs to my room and showed me how to wear the jock strap by stepping into it and pulling it up a little way over his pants. The important thing to show was that the cup went in the front. He stepped out of it and handed it back. I shucked my shorts and underwear then and there and donned the jock before Mike could leave, just to make sure I did it correctly. I wanted everything surrounding my football career to start off on the right foot. Mike nodded his approval, suppressed a smile, and left the room. I was all set in the personal protective equipment department. I wore it for the rest of the day. So began my auspicious start.

My exciting dream of scoring touchdowns was short-lived. It died on the practice field soon after the season began. The game was very different from the front yard games I'd played in the neighborhood. This was organized Texas schoolboy football, and even on the seventh-grade level, it was fast and rough. Everything was taken very seriously. My diminutive size quickly relegated me to fourth-string, where I was listed as quarterback. My chances of getting into any games were nil, except for when the team was far ahead and only a few seconds remained on the clock. The other fourth-string scrubs and I always left the games with the cleanest uniforms.

Practices were a different story. Third and fourth stringers on the team were so much fodder for the first and second-stringers. We were tackling dummies and were ground upon mercilessly. If I thought going against second-stringers might be easier than the first-string starters, I was mistaken. The second-stringers were the desperate ones, on the cusp and so close to being first-string. Any chance to stand out by running over, blocking, or tackling a fourth-stringer was done with fury. The third and fourth-stringers also role-played as players from the upcoming opponents who had been scouted as to what offensive and defensive schemes they ran. The first- and second-stringers either drove down the field on the hapless role-playing defenders, or played smothering, vicious defense when the third and fourth-stringers were acting as the opponent's offense. Virtually any time I threw a forward pass I was intercepted. The goal for the ragtag scrubs and me became simple survival. I was covered in bumps, scrapes, and bruises. Quitting, however, was unthinkable.

I usually rode home in the backseat of the station wagon after a game, sullen and crestfallen over not getting a chance to play. My mother would give me permission to cry, but I resolutely would not. I knew Lou Gehrig never cried.

Once, I did get into a game with several minutes left on the clock, playing defensive back. Usually the games I got into were like blurs to me, things happened so fast. On one particular play that day, however, I saw things unfolding with crystal clarity. A long pass was coming down toward the receiver I was covering. I suddenly realized I was actually in the right position to make an interception. My pupils dilated, heartbeats increased, and everything else fell away as I saw the ball floating down directly toward me. It was like slow motion. I planted myself and began to reach up to welcome the errant pass into my arms. But just as the football fell into my waiting arms, my vision was suddenly crowded with half a dozen other reaching hands. I was in the middle of a convergence of bodies. The ball tipped from hand to hand for a moment, including mine, before falling harmlessly incomplete as we all fell to the ground. But I had touched the ball. At game's end I trotted off the field feeling like a warrior. My white football pants even boasted a grass stain.

At school the next day I was still giddy with the experience. During lunchtime recess on the blacktop, I stood with a group of teammates talking about the game. Excitedly, I caught the attention of one of the boys. "Didja see I almost had that interception?"

"No," the other boy replied tersely. "You didn't almost get nothin'."

"I did too!" I said indignantly. "Even Matt and Dave said they saw me. Cecil Phelps even said 'good play'!"

"Bullshit," the other boy said.

I suddenly understood why the boy was denying the play so adamantly. He had been the one I was sent in to replace during the game, and he resented being pulled for a fourth-stringer. I turned and walked off, determined not to let that kid tarnish my memory. I had so few chances to play. I cherished every moment.

But Cecil Phelps had indeed acknowledged me. He was a first-string running back, one of a handful of starting Black players. He was well built and strong and the fastest player on the team. He was an electrifying runner in the open field. I loved watching him run and score touchdowns. Cecil even gave me a soul handshake after the game.

For the most part, though, it was not what I had envisioned for myself and my cherished dream. Things were as difficult in the locker room as they were on the field. Every boy on the team had his assigned place in the pecking order. By the time that order reached me, there were no others below. Some of the boys occupied the same rung on the ladder I did, but it was the lowest rung. The teasing and bullying went unchecked. To the coaches it was part of how teams became cohesive and functional. Everyone had their place. Even at the seventh-grade level, it was about winning.

Kevin Bard was the unquestioned leader of the team. He was the tallest member of the team by far. At twelve years old, he was already six feet tall. That seventh grade year team pictures from any of the sports, football, basketball or track was a comical thing to look at. Kevin was always in the middle of the back row, a sudden spike standing head and shoulders above the rest. I would be somewhere along the front line, dwarfed by the ones around me, head down, looking up at the camera from under my eyebrows.

Kevin held sway over all the other players; it didn't matter if they were White or Black. He and his posse ruled the locker room with impunity. He pegged me the very first time he saw me getting dressed for the first practice.

"Hey, queerbait," he said derisively. "You can carry my jockstrap for me, okay?"

I had virtually melted into the floor at the mention of that name. The dreaded thought, *Does he really know about camp?* flooded my mind.

There was no way Kevin could have known anything about my summer. Our worlds were too far apart. That fact didn't occur to me. The name pierced my heart. I stood at my locker, silent.

Kevin stood up and advanced toward me, sensing a weakling. He came up very close, pinning me back against the locker. I didn't even reach chest height on him. I looked up into Kevin's menacing face.

"I said, ya wanna carry my jockstrap, peckerhead?" he sneered as he looked down at me.

I swallowed hard and said nothing. Suddenly, Kevin lifted a knee and drove it straight into my groin. Looking upward, I never saw it coming. I collapsed in a heap, holding my testicles. I tried not to burst into tears, but I couldn't help it.

"Crybaby," he sneered again and walked away.

It was pretty much the only time the starters paid any attention to the bottom-feeding fourth-stringers. When they felt like having fun at someone's expense, the fourth-stringers fit the bill. Race didn't matter. This was the world of male athletics. We did the best we could to defend ourselves, but we were on their own. A code of silence forbade going to the coaches to complain about being picked on. Occasionally, if a coach witnessed such treatment that went beyond the pale, he would try to even the score by giving the poor fourth-stringer an opportunity to directly oppose their antagonist during tackling drills. However, such mismatches invariably meant simply another pounding into the dirt by the bigger, faster star.

"Atta boy!" the coach would say in praise to the victor. "Way to stick 'em!"

I once had an opportunity to try to bring Kevin down in a tackling drill. He bore down on me, carrying the ball tucked under his arm, and simply ran me over. I managed to cling to his foot for a few yards before falling harmlessly away.

"Atta boy, Kevin!" the coach yelled. He paused to spit a huge wad of tobacco juice. Wiping his mouth with the back of his hand, he yelled again. "Next! C'mon, let's go here! Show some hustle, gentlemen!"

And so for the next three years, my athletic experience fell into seasonal patterns that measured the passing of time as I followed the lead of the school's elite athletes. I thought of the seasons not as fall, winter, spring, or summer, but as football, basketball, track, and vacation. It gave me a sense of order and belonging, handicapped as I was by my small frame, which invariably made me a perennial benchwarmer in a uniform that was always too big for me. But I had a purpose. I wore a constant mosaic of lumps and bruises from season to season as I grimly held to my role as fodder for the better kids to practice on. In eighth grade I played just a little more in the football games. In track I became the 880 and mile runner. By the time ninth-grade football came around, I had managed to fight my way up to second-string. I was still on the small side, but I was quick, and my coaches admired my determination. A lot of the seventh and eigth-grade third and fourth-stringers had fallen by the wayside and never showed up for another season of pounding punishment. I showed up every year.

<hr>

It is said in Texas there are two sports, football and spring football. I had a good regular season during the fall of ninth grade. I was beginning to develop as an athlete and even growing a bit. I was still on the small side, but three years as a scrub had toughened me and honed my quickness and agility, if for nothing else but simple survival. That fall I saw increased playing time and even scored my first touchdown in a game. Both my parents were there to see it.

The season was going well for the team and at the end of September we were undefeated. Spirits were high. On October 2nd however, the collective heart of football throughout the entire town was tragically broken by news of the plane crash carrying half of the Wichita State University football team enroute to Utah for a game. Two hometown athletes, former standout Bearcats, were on the plane.

News filtered in as the town held its breath. Mike Bruce, the Bearcat's former rugged defensive end, stumbled and crawled bleeding down the mountainside in search of help for his teammates. Johnny Taylor, the former Bearcat star quarteback lay severly burned in the wreckage of the plane. I heard Colleen in her bedroom crying one evening for the young man who was a friend and occasional date. I could remember Johnny at our house.

Over the next few weeks during home games the public adress announcer would take a moment at halftime to say a brief word about Johnny as he lay in a hospital bed fighting for his life. The announcer's tone was soft and somber. Not a sound could be heard throughout the stadium as everything stopped for a moment. I could feel the emotional weight of the crowd as we wore a heavy heart.

Finally, one chilly and windy autumn day, the headline in the newspaper finished the job of breaking the town's heart. A huge headline with only two words ran across the top of the front page. TAYLOR SUCCUMBS.

Both junior highs and Frederick Douglas High sent members of their football teams to the graveside funeral service at the West Hill Cemetery on a bright fall day. I stood at the periphery, watching solemnly. I saw Mike Bruce, standing with crutches and weeping unabashedly for his friend. Many wept alongside him for the young man who would forever remain the smiling, dark haired handsome man in the high school yearbook. It was the saddest day I could remember.

In the spring of my ninth-grade year I looked forward to my first experience with spring football with a mix of excited anticipation and a lingering dread. For the spring football season was overseen not just by the junior high school coaching staff, but the high school coaches as well. Both of the junior high schools in town, Dillingham and Piner, were sending their ninth-grade players. It was the transition to the high school level. This meant not only increased competition for recognition and playing time, but for me, it also meant the possibility of encountering Paul, Chris, Joey, Robbie, and Billy Swift again. I had had little contact with any of them in almost three years. The prospect was unnerving for me.

Two things occurred to turn the spring season into a positive, seminal event in my life. The first was that upon the initial meeting between the players blended together from what had heretofore been bitter archrivals, I saw no sign of any of the boys from the neighborhood. The intervening years had led the others from their singular focus on football that summer after the sixth grade into other pursuits. I was secretly relieved and thus able to give undivided attention to the customary ritual of sizing up the others. The boys from each school had been teammates and knew each other for three years. Now, we were in a room together with a whole new group of boys. The sizing up proceeded subtly and earnestly.

I recollected Stevie Walsh's stories about the games he'd played in between Dillingham and Piner during his junior high days, in which invariably the noble and good Dillingham had routinely been victorious. When I reached junior high, I found that not to be the case. When we gathered that spring in my ninth-grade year for our first meeting as prospective new teammates, the Piner boys came knowing that in three years we had never once lost to Dillingham. We entered the meeting as ones who knew how to win. I thoroughly enjoyed it.

The second great occurrence to befall me came from a most unlikely benefactor. Eileen, my bossy, babysitting sister. She had graduated from high school when I entered the ninth grade and left for college at East Texas State. The skills she honed keeping four boys in line blended with an education that would, in time, turn her into the first-class teacher she would become. Somewhere along the line in her first year at school, she met her future husband, a native Texan, who happened to be a coach over at Dillingham and who had played his college football in Texas. He had played well enough, in fact, to be invited to try out with an NFL team. He was viewed as a god by my entire family the very first time my sister had brought him home to meet us. Tall, blond, and blue-eyed, he was the quintessential wide receiver; strong, fast, and graceful. He never left our home without throwing at least fifty passes to all us boys. We adored him. He was also going to be one of the coaches for the spring football season.

The players from the two schools were blended and organized into different positions. I was designated as a wide receiver along with six or seven others. None other than my future brother-in-law would coach us. I felt it to be a stroke of great luck, which it turned out to be.

I was smart enough not to flaunt my connection to the others. My sister's fiancé paid me no more attention during practice than he did the others. I competed for time and attention just the same as all the rest of the athletes.

After practice one afternoon, I was walking toward the field house and the showers, straggling along behind the rest of the players. It had been a tough practice for me. I couldn't seem to catch the ball all practice long. I had dropped several long passes when I was clearly in the open. I was dejected, dirty, and cross with myself.

I heard Carlton, my sister's fiancé, behind me on the field calling my name. I turned around to see what he wanted. He waved me back over to the field.

When I reached him he was very businesslike. He was a science teacher at Dillingham and so was a natural teacher who knew how to take charge.

"We're going to work a little bit here on your receiving skills," he said. "I want you to stand downfield about fifteen yards. I'm going to throw you some passes. I want you to listen to what I say."

"Yes, sir," I replied. I trotted off fifteen yards and turned around to look at my coach.

He fired a pass at me, which I caught in my belly. I juggled it for a moment before dropping it to the ground. Embarrassed, I angrily picked the ball up and fired it back.

"Ya see what you're doing?" Carlton said. I shook my head. "You're tryin' to catch the ball with your body. Catch it with your hands, in front of you like this." He held the ball out in front of him, his big hands clasped around it. He shook it to emphasize his point.

"In front of you, with your hands. Then you bring it into your body like this." He brought the ball down slowly under his arm. "The whole time you're watching it with your eyes. All the way till you tuck it away." He demonstrated again, emphasizing the movement of his head and eyes following his hands as he slowly tucked the ball away. "Catch with the hands. Watch it all the way under your arm. That's how you catch a football. Try it again."

He threw the ball slowly at me. I diligently reached out in front of me and caught it with my hands. With my eyes locked on it, I tucked the ball under my arm.

"That's right," he said. "Let's do it some more."

After a dozen or so successful tries, Carlton held the ball. "Now, let's run some routes. I want you to do a deep post pattern. I'll throw you the ball."

I trotted out along a scrimmage line to a spot a wide receiver would normally position himself. Carlton held the ball in front of him and simulated taking a snap from center. I took off down the field, executed a smart cut at fifteen yards, and angled in at a forty-five-degree angle toward the goal post at the end of the field. I looked back and saw the ball high in the air sailing downfield toward a spot where I was supposed to converge with the ball. Desperate, I threw my arms out in front of me and continued to run to the spot I knew I had to be to make the catch. I never got there. The ball hit the ground several yards in front of me.

"No, no, no!" Carlton cried loudly. "You don't run your route with your arms out in front of you like that! It just slows you down and robs your speed. You'll never shake your defender running like that!"

Frustrated, I trotted back to my coach and tossed him the ball. "You don't reach for the ball until you can grab it," he said emphatically. "You gotta time it. Let's do some more."

I ran several more deep routes, remembering what I was being taught. One of my strong suits was a willingness to be coached and to learn quickly. It didn't take long at all before I was flying downfield, making a cut, and being patient enough to wait for the ball to arrive at the point where all I had to do was reach out and grab it in the air with my hands and bring it into my body, following it with my eyes till it was tucked away.

"There ya go, son," Carlton said after a dozen routes down the field. "You got it. One other thing. Carry a ball in your hands at home every chance you get. Sleep with it." He smiled at me. "Now hit the showers."

I ran off, feeling elated with my newfound skills. A football became my constant companion at home and my nightly companion in bed.

The spring season culminated after a month of practice with the annual intrasquad scrimmage, held in the town stadium. Although it was merely a controlled scrimmage with the coaches out on the field along with the players coaching and acting as referees, the stands were filled with people anxious to evaluate the next crop of Bearcats. The local newspaper was there snapping pictures. Football is king.

I was part of the junior varsity team, which played ahead of the varsity. I had never seen so many people in the stands at any of my junior high games. This was the big time. It was exciting to behold.

I didn't score any touchdowns that day, but I remembered what I was taught and made several good catches during the game. I was very satisfied with my performance and vowed to practice diligently all summer long. In a life of fragile balance, fraught with self-doubt and bleak feelings of inadequacy, a life led walking around on egg shells waiting for someone to shout "queerbait!" in my direction, it was vital to be able to succeed in one important place. I knew how to catch a football. I discovered a whole new love for my sister.

THE YEAR OF TREPIDATION

"...'Tis I'll be there in sunshine or in shadow...
...Or when the valley's hushed and white with snow..."

The entire circumference of the road that circled our neighbor-hood was a little more than a half mile long. My father and I had driven it in the car, measuring the distance with the odometer.

I began to run the circle to keep my conditioning over the summer after my ninth-grade year so that I'd be prepared for the tenth grade and junior varsity football. After dinner each evening when the heat of the day had broken, I put on sneakers, cutoff shorts, and a hand-me-down tee shirt and ran the circle. In short order I was doing six laps nightly. When I was done running I would go inside and lift weights in the guest room with my Sears & Roebuck junior weight set. I could feel myself getting stronger. I carried a football everywhere I went.

One evening as I rounded the corner at the bottom of the neigh-borhood I looked up and saw Stevie Walsh, Paul, Chris, and Joey standing around Stevie's car parked on the side of the road. They stopped talking as I approached on the other side of the road. I kept my eyes forward.

"Hey," Stevie said, "looky who's comin' by!" He stood up from leaning against his car and started walking across the road. The others followed.

I noticed that Stevie had changed after graduating from high school the year before. He hadn't gone on to college. A year of sitting home on the couch without a job, eating peanut butter and fluff sandwiches as he watched television all day had put weight around his middle and had given him a double chin. I picked up my pace a little.

"Whoa," Stevie said in a ringleader tone. "Where ya goin' so fast? Stop an' say howdy!" The others laughed. They stopped in the road and stood in my way. I stopped short, wanting at first to just veer around them, but then not wanting to seem like I was afraid of them either. Stevie sure looked out of shape, but he was still bigger than me and four years older.

"Hey, guys," I said warily as I stopped.

"I seen ya runnin' every evenin'," Stevie said. "Guess ya wanna be a Bearcat, huh?"

"Somethin' like that," I replied. "I gotta keep runnin'. See ya." I went to step around the others and resume running.

Stevie jumped out in my way. "Hold on a sec," he said, holding a hand out and stopping me. "We didn't say ya could leave yet. We wanna know how a queerbait thinks he's gotta chance to be a Bearcat. They don't take pecker-eaters on the team."

The others laughed uproariously. "Hahahaha," Chris roared. "Queerbaits playin' football. That's stupid!"

"I don't see you out there," I shot back, glowering at Chris.

"Shut up, peckerhead," Stevie said, low and dangerous. He kept his hand up in front of me.

I looked at Stevie. "Fuck you," I said. Impulsively, I slapped Stevie's hand away from in front of me, stepped around him, and began running.

"Sonuvabitch!" Stevie snarled. "Come back here, ya little twerp." He spun and started running after me.

I looked over my shoulder and saw Stevie bearing down on me. The other boys were giving chase as well. I turned back around and gave a burst of speed. I ran about twenty-five yards and looked back again. My speed surprised them. Stevie was infuriated.

"Ya motherfucker," he snarled. "I'm gonna catch you." He started running harder.

I turned around and gave an even greater burst and began tearing down the road. Looking back, I saw Stevie and the others falling farther behind. Stevie was still in front, but his playing days were long over, and he'd spent too many hours on the couch. He began to look winded. I knew I had the race won, but I was still afraid. I didn't want to chance a fight with any one of them, especially Stevie. Stevie might be getting fat, but he was still strong. I had been in exactly two fights in my life, not counting the daily skirmishes with my brothers. I had no heart for it. It made my knees wobbly.

I continued to run hard till I turned the next corner and headed back up the long hill we all used to ride our go-carts down a lifetime ago. Looking back, I saw no sign of them. I slowed to my normal running pace. I should've felt victorious after outrunning all of them, but I didn't. I was afraid.

I turned the corner at the top of the long, gentle hill and began to head for home. It would cut the run short, but I didn't care. I didn't want to see them again. I was still four or five houses away from home when I looked up at the noise of squealing tires to see Stevie's car headed my way. I stopped where I was and watched his car approach.

Stevie stopped short just in front of me and jumped out along with the others. They walked toward me, angry as hornets.

"Thought ya could get away so fast, huh?" Stevie sneered. "Get 'im Paul."

I saw Paul come toward me swinging his right fist. I took an involuntary step backward, but Paul still managed to graze my chin. I reached out blindly to grab him. Chris stepped forward and hooked a punch to my shoulder. Suddenly mad, I swung back and connected with the side of Chris's head.

"Yeeoww!" Chris cried. "Ya little twerp! Dang!"

Paul and I grappled with each other and fell to the pavement wrestling. Chris went to kick me, but missed and struck Paul in the leg.

"Oooofff!" Paul said. "Ya little snot!"

"I didn't mean it!" Chris said. "I's tryin' to get *him!*"

Paul and I continued wrestling on the ground. Although I was holding my own against him, I was crying. I hated fighting. Stevie circled us.

"Get 'im in a leg lock and a Nelson so's I can fuckin' give 'im a punch!" he said. He was still breathing hard.

"Hey!" a loud voice called out. "What's going on!"

Everyone stopped and looked over at Mr. Stevens standing in the front door of his home. Hearing the ruckus, he'd put down his paper and pipe and went to investigate the kerfuffle in front of his home. No one said a word.

He looked at the two boys on the ground. "You two get up off the street," he said. "All you boys head home now or I'm going to start calling some parents. I know who each one of you are."

"Yes, sir," came a sullen, chorused reply.

Paul and I got up, each checking our scrapes from the asphalt. Stevie started back for his car with Chris and Joey.

"C'mon," he said, "let's get outta here."

Mr. Stevens turned and went back inside. I stood there, gingerly touching a scrape on the outside of an elbow. Stevie started the car up and swung out around me. Paul stuck his head out the window of the front seat. Chris was looking out from behind him in the backseat.

"Jus' remember, queerbait," Paul said darkly, "we're gonna be in the tenth grade too an' everyone's gonna know you're a dick sucker."

"Yeah!" Chris sang out from the backseat. "Everyone's gonna know!"

They drove off and disappeared around the corner. I stood there in the street, not knowing what to do. I was still crying. Thinking about going into the tenth grade now made me cry even more. I would be alone again going into a new school, just as I had done at Piner. I had no sweetheart. There was no best friend for a pal. I stood there in the gathering dusk crying to myself. I did not start for home till I had cried myself dry.

⟸⟹

Tenth grade started, and I stepped into the new high school on tenterhooks, looking for any sign of any of the boys from my neighborhood. It was a great relief to find I shared no classes with any of them. Occasionally I would see one of them from a distance. I would quickly look away and walk off in another direction or duck between rows of lockers. I heard no hateful names hurled in my direction.

Football started, drawing most of my attention. I was fighting for a starting spot, which I found frustrating. Despite my success the previous spring and the shape I was in at the beginning of school, I found that reputations had preceded almost all the athletes from both junior high schools, both for the starters and the scrubs.

Almost from the beginning the first and second-string players mirrored those from junior high, with a scattering of others from Dillingham. I found myself listed at third-string before the start of the very first practice. It would be tough going for me to get any playing time.

There were other things, though, to assuage my frustrations on the football field. Suddenly, the girls looked very grown-up and even more exciting to look at. I still had to remain vigilant to adjust myself when necessary, or when that was impossible, to either remain seated or carry my books in front of my waist.

As if being immersed in a world where the girls seemed so alluring and my imagination was busy inventing a world full of possibilities weren't enough, I obtained my driver's license at the beginning of November when I turned sixteen. I had completed Drivers Ed during the summer and had my learner's permit, but being sixteen meant two things; having my license and the ability to date.

My parents had designated sixteen as the age of consent as far as dating was concerned. It had bought them some time to prepare when my two sisters were approaching that magical milestone. They had needed it, given their daughters' precociousness and a parent's natural fear of the unknown when they have teenage children. Now it was their firstborn son's turn.

I took the family car down to DMV on my sixteenth birthday, which was a Tuesday. I had permission from my parents as a birthday gift to miss the first class of the day and be at the licensing bureau when it opened in the morning. I was then allowed to take the car to school.

I drove into the school parking lot, my new license carefully situated in my wallet, and feeling like a man of the world. I hooked an elbow out the window as I drove slowly by a group of girls in the wood-paneled family station wagon. I was grinning like a goof.

Later that morning I walked right up to Vicki McDuffy and asked her out on a date for that Saturday. She said yes. After football practice that afternoon, I had driven straight home and announced my plans at the dinner table.

"I have a date this Saturday," I said very importantly.

"Really?" Timmy asked, keen with interest. He was in the ninth grade now and was fully immersed in his own throes of adolescence.

"No, you don't," my father said matter-of-factly.

My head swirled in his direction. "But you said I could date when I got my license!" I wailed. I could feel myself reverting to a small child asking for some candy. I was getting smaller. I had made my announcement in front of my brothers. I had an image to uphold, and my father was obliterating it.

"Nope," my father said simply.

"You said I could date when I turned sixteen and got my license!" I said hotly. "An' I already asked Vicki McDuffy out!" My face was flushed.

My father said nothing and continued to eat his dinner. There was a silence around the table.

"Dear," my mother said after a moment, looking at her husband from the other end of the table.

My father looked back at her for a moment. Then he smiled and chuckled. "I was only kidding," he said, smiling at me. "Sorry."

Enormous relief, then, "Can I have ten bucks? We're goin' to the drive-in!"

I had a night to remember. I had dressed to the nines and showed up at Vicki's exactly when I said I would. Her father had answered the door and asked the usual suspicious questions. Fortunately, her father was also a football fan, so he didn't give me too hard a time. Most of the questions centered on the current football season.

We got to the drive-in, picked our spot off to the side near the back, and promptly got into the backseat.

"There's something I want you to do," Vicki said demurely.

"Yeah?" I said, barely daring to imagine the possibilities. I was breathless.

She ducked her head smiling. "Something," she repeated. "Guess."

"Umm, well," I stammered. My heart would not stop pounding. "What?"

"Guess."

"Well," I began. I didn't want to blow things by saying something way out of bounds and upsetting her. "Uh, I can think of three things." I looked up as someone passed the car. My head was swimming. The movie was beginning. I had no idea what it was.

"What three things?"

"Umm, ah," I had to say something. Quickly I blurted,

"French-kissin', givin' a hickey, or coppin' a feel." There, I'd said it. All three of those things were all at the top of my imagination. Any one of those was the acme of possibilities for me.

"Yeah," she said. "That one."

"Which one?" The game was maddening to me.

"The second one," she replied.

My mind reeled with the thought. I'd seen hickeys at school. Everyone knew that anyone with a hickey at school or wearing a turtleneck after a weekend date was practically "doing it."

"The first one too," Vicki said. "I only French-kissed once."

"Yeah, me too," I lied.

The cool autumn air floated against the windows of the car, warmed by the breathless exhalations of knife-edge teenage emotion. The resulting fogging provided the cover necessary to proceed. She unbuttoned the first two buttons of her blouse, revealing smooth, creamy skin. Tentatively, I reached a hand gently around the back of her neck and leaned forward to kiss her. Colors exploded in my head. Awkwardly, gently, we touched each other's tongues with our own, adolescent curiosity carrying us aloft. She tasted delicious. Instantly, the most intense erection I ever had launched in my pants. I moved down her neck, lingering to explore the warm skin. I could feel her pulse there. I inhaled her sweet, clean scent. After a moment, I moved down a little more to the top of her open blouse, which still modestly covered her breasts, and proceeded to apply a hickey just like I had practiced in the past after noticing one on my sister's neck and asking her how they got there. She had shown my brothers and me by demonstrating the process on the inside of her forearm. For weeks afterward, we boys had self-applied hickeys covering our forearms till Mother commanded that we halt. It was a cardinal sin against the church, she said.

I had her home promptly after the movie. We didn't linger long in front of her house. We knew we were being watched.

"I'll show you the results at school," she told me. She leaned over and gave me a quick kiss. I watched her walk in through her front door. Then, looking down at my watch, I saw I was twenty minutes past my mother's curfew. Panicked, I ran back to the car, jumped in, and dropped it into drive and sped off.

I arrived home, flying into the garage, fortunate to not hit anything, and parked. I closed my eyes, hoping my mother wouldn't be too angry. Suddenly, the entire garage was filled with a thick, white, and acrid-smelling smoke. Panicking again, I wondered what was wrong. Was something on fire? I looked around the car, then down at the floor under the dash. *Where was it coming from?* I thought as I started to cough.

My eye caught the emergency brake pedal. It was planted all the way down to the floorboard. I quickly pulled the release lever. It snapped back into the released position. I got out of the car and headed for the utility room door, waving my hand in front of me.

My mother was on the couch in the den watching Johnny Carson on the television. "How was your date?" she asked pleasantly.

"Umm, fine," I replied and started to walk away.

"What movie did you see?"

"Umm, *Billy Jack*."

She started to say something, then stopped. She wrinkled her nose. "Ugh," Mother said. "What's that awful smell?"

I shrugged. "I dunno."

"Is something burning?"

"Umm, I don't think so."

"Phew," she said getting up. "Better close some windows before we go to bed."

"'Kay," I said.

We hastily shut some windows and went off to our rooms. I lay awake, reliving the night's magic and smelling my date's perfume on my hands until it faded away.

The rest of the fall heading into Christmas was a mixed bag of pleasure, pain, and new experiences for me. Football continued to be a struggle. I loved the higher echelon of the junior varsity level with its night games and greater attendance by the townspeople. I chafed, however, at the lack of playing time. I believed in my heart I was better than both the first and second-string wide receivers, but the caste system was rigid. Barring injury or exhaustion, first and second-stringers played the majority of the time.

Dating was exciting, though no steady girlfriend emerged. I found it hard sometimes to work up the nerve each week to ask a girl out. A date every weekend was the social norm to achieve and maintain. A steady girlfriend, I thought, would've helped in that department.

I did have a small cadre of friends to share lunch periods, a few classes, and the bench during football games with. To anyone watching, my life appeared to be what it was meant to be for a sixteen year old; carefree, fun, with problems no more dangerous than too much homework, pimples, having a car, and money to put gas in it with or being the butt of a joke in front of others. Those things concerned me too, but always, always, I walked cautiously through the hallways, looking for any sign of the other neighborhood boys I knew I might encounter at any time.

That winter there was a death at school, the first such experience for me. A boy from my homeroom class died suddenly from an unknown medical malady. The homeroom teacher, Mr. Holcombe, a young man with long sideburns and who had a strong country boy streak in him, announced the news in hushed tones during class. The kid had been a very quiet one, a small skinny Black kid who sat toward the back of the class. I remembered once exchanging a glance and a small smile with him, but I never heard him speak and could barely remember his face. He had been another one of the invisible poor who quietly haunted the school.

As I happened to be standing around Mr. Holcomb's desk shortly after the announcement, he looked at me and said suddenly, "It would be appropriate to make some sort of gesture to the family, don't you think?"

"Umm, sure," I replied, surprised Mr. Holcombe was directing his remarks to me. "Like what?"

"I don't know," Mr. Holcombe replied, frowning. He thought for a moment. "Maybe we should represent the school at the funeral. It's the day after tomorrow."

"Who?" I said.

"How 'bout us two?" he replied. He looked at a girl who happened to be standing nearby. "An' maybe Candy too."

Candy looked at us both upon hearing her name. "Huh?" she said.

"Would you like to go with us to represent the school at the funeral?"

She looked puzzled. "Do what?"

Mr. Holcombe explained. "I'm sure I could get permission from the school for us to attend the funeral to pay respects on behalf of the school. Would you like to go?"

Candy resided at the upper echelons of high school society. Pretty, vivacious, and wide-eyed, she sensed an opportunity to stand out.

"Umm, sure," she said flashing a bright smile. "What do I wear?"

"Uh, dress appropriately for a funeral," Mr. Holcombe deadpanned. He looked at me. "Whatta ya say?"

"Sure," I replied. "I got a suit I can wear."

"Good," Mr. Holcombe said. "I'll make the arrangements with the school. We'll be going Wednesday morning."

I tried to appear grown-up about the situation, but I was very intrigued at the prospect of spending time alongside one of the school's most popular girls and attending a funeral, neither of which I'd ever done before.

Wednesday morning arrived grey and cool. Mr. Holcombe pulled in front of the school in a Dodge pickup, where his two students were waiting outside the main entrance. I was dressed in my only suit, an off-white, double-breasted, wide-collared ensemble with a striped purple shirt and a wide, white tie, and white shoes. I loved the suit and had picked it out myself at Montgomery Ward. Candy was dressed in a stunning red and white miniskirt, which I also loved. Mr. Holcombe was in his rather ordinary teacher attire, a powder blue suit coat and tie.

It took Mr. Holcombe a long time to get to the church. We were very far out into the countryside when at last we came over a rise and spotted the simple, worn-looking building. It was a plain, cinderblock structure with a peaked roof and small steeple that leaned a little.

The parking area was a hard packed, red dirt lot filled with old-looking cars and pickup trucks. Mr. Holcombe found a spot at the far end from where we came in and parked. He looked around.

"We'll just go in and find a place to sit," he said. "Not sure how these Baptists do things. Remember to be polite."

Candy and I nodded our heads. She looked very apprehensive.

"Is this a Black church?" she asked.

"Yes, Candy," Mr. Holcombe replied. "It's a Black church. You okay?"

"Um, I guess," she said nervously. "Where do the White people sit?"

"Everybody sits together here," he said. "Alright?"

Candy hesitated, looking out the truck window toward the front door of the church at some of the congregation members making their way in.

"Um, I guess," she said again quietly.

"How 'bout you?" he said looking at me.

"Uh-huh," I said nodding. "I'm okay."

"Good. Let's go."

We entered the crowded church through the front door and stood there looking around. I could see we were the only White people there. I saw ladies dressed in their best, with white gloves and hats. I saw Black men in farmer's overalls and a few of them in dark suits, old and threadbare.

With Mr. Holcombe's blue suit coat, Candy's stylish miniskirt, and my off-white ensemble we stood out. Our clothes shouted with modern colors and styles in a worn-out, black-and-white world. I felt very conspicuous.

An older, dignified-looking gentleman approached us and shook hands with Mr. Holcombe, speaking quietly with him as Candy and I looked around. People were milling about, hugging each other. There was a lot of talking going on. Occasionally a loud wail broke out, startling Candy and me.

I looked toward the front of the church and saw a plain wooden pulpit off to one side. In the middle was an open casket. In the casket lay the small skinny boy I had never spoken to, but remembered more clearly now. I stared at the boy lying so still. I had never seen a dead person before.

Mr. Holcombe interrupted my reverie. "It's time to take a seat," he said. "Follow me."

We sat down about halfway to the front as the service began. The service was completely beyond the realm of anything I had ever experienced in church before. There were constant outbursts from the congregation as the preacher extolled the resurrection of Christ, the joys of righteous living, the approaching Rapture and Day of Judgment. Amens and hallelujahs rang out, which constantly startled Candy and me. Our heads swiveled from side to side as folks called out. Sudden, loud wailing would erupt from both men and women.

I had never experienced such an expression of raw emotion before.

At the end of the service the preacher invited everyone down the aisle to view the departed one more time. Mr. Holcombe rose from his seat as our turn came and gestured to us to follow. I elbowed Candy gently.

"Wanna go see the body?" I whispered.

Candy shook her head. "No," she said as she looked down at her feet.

I got up and walked down the aisle alongside Mr. Holcombe. We stopped and waited our turn to approach. When it came, we stepped forward, hands clasped in front of us. Being so close to a dead body utterly fascinated me. I kept staring at how still the boy in the casket was. He looked like the kid from homeroom, I thought, but his stillness made me wonder. I'd never seen such stillness. I thought, *Is it really him?*

Afterward, I sat lost in thought in the pickup on our way back to school. The kid was really dead. I'd heard of kids getting killed before, getting electrocuted or drowning or something. Death was such a mysterious thing. I thought, *How could someone who just looks like they're sleeping be dead?* Mr. Holcombe had said something about a lump behind one of the boy's ears. Really? Could just a plain old lump make a kid dead? Involuntarily, my hand went to the back of my head, fingers gingerly touching the area behind my ear.

I thought often of the boy I'd hardly known from my homeroom during the rest of the year. It was strange to me how someone could be living one moment, someone I had actually exchanged a smile with, and then be dead. I wondered what it was like to be dead. It made me shudder.

⇥⬥⬦

During track that spring, I began a running argument with another boy who had also once been a boyfriend of Susan Whisman during junior high. The other boy talked about how easy she as we sat around stretching before practice.

"I did her a hundred times," he had boasted with a sly wink and a crooked smile to the others. They all laughed and believed him. I never did. I knew better and would say so.

Annoyed, he finally said to me at practice one day, "What's your deal anyways?"

"Jus' quit talkin' 'bout her that way," I shot back. "She was nice."

He looked away. "She was a slut," he said dismissively.

I launched myself off the ground and landed on him. I got in a couple of quick punches before we tied each other up and began rolling on the ground wrestling for an advantage. Immediately a crowd formed around us.

After a minute the coach broke through blowing his whistle. He hauled both of us off the ground.

"That's it, boys," he drawled.

"He started it," the other boy accused. "He jus' came after me. Little queerbait."

My mind went white-hot at the name. I lunged at him. "Shut up!" I screeched. "Just shut up!"

"That's enough!" the coach bellowed. "Both of you, start doin' laps, now. The rest of you! Get back to yer places!"

Still fuming, I walked off toward the track. I'd had enough of queerbait. And I'd had enough of this punk's talk of a girl I would always love. I reached the track and took off running, just to be away from everyone.

After track season another round of spring football began. At that time class schedules for the following year also came out. Students spent days comparing schedules, seeing which classes they got into, which popular kids or friends, cute girls or boys were in class with them, and what teachers they had. The demographics were very important.

I stood at my locker one morning, comparing schedules with another kid on the football team. I was expressing uneasiness over my assignment to Mr. Peters's algebra class. Mr. Peters had a reputation for being strict and giving lots of homework. Suddenly, Paul and Joey poked their heads from around a nearby corner.

"Hey, pecker breath," Joey said. "Ya got old man Peters, huh? Guess what? So do we!"

I swallowed. It felt like a stone going down inside me. I stared wordlessly at them.

"Should be a good time!" Paul joined in. "Right, Joey?" He gave Joey an elbow to the ribs.

"You betcha!" Joey replied.

"Friends of yours?" the teammate asked.

"No," I said. I closed my locker.

"Hell, yeah, we are," Joey said. "We used to go to camp together!" He gave me a big wink.

I abruptly turned and walked away, shame flushing my cheeks. Looking back over my shoulder I saw Paul and Joey engaged in an animated discussion with my teammate. My heart sank in my chest. I knew what they were talking about. I felt as if the last refuge I had, the football team, was about to be destroyed.

I thought about going to the office to ask for a class reassignment. But then again, I thought, what if they ask why? I had no idea what I could say to fix that dilemma. I rounded a corner and stopped, leaning up against the wall. It was just so unfair, I thought. I leaned my head back and closed my eyes. This was it, I thought. The whole world is going to know.

"Everything okay, son?"

I looked up to see Mr. Bowden, the PE teacher, walking by and looking at me.

"Yes, sir," I replied and walked off.

AWAY

"...'Tis you, 'tis you must go and I must hide..."

I sat with my brothers around the dinner table, parents at both ends. It was the beginning of May. The previous NFL football season was long over, but still the dinnertime conversation centered on the first Super Bowl victory of the Dallas Cowboys the previous January over the Miami Dolphins. The victory had erased all previous disappointments suffered by our favorite football team. No more frozen defeat in Green Bay. No more disasters against Cleveland. No more heartbreak over the first Super Bowl appearance, a loss to the Colts. The Super Bowl win made the cold, brown winter practically cheerful.

Lately I had been more reserved than usual, allowing my brothers the majority of the daily din and noise of family life. Inwardly, I felt like a prisoner awaiting my fate. The thought of my upcoming junior year and the certain disaster waiting to happen sapped my spirit. I was quiet, ate little, and worked out without enthusiasm.

"What's the matter with you lately?" Mother asked me once. "Worried about football next year?"

I shrugged. "Nothin'," I said.

Mother and Father looked at each other across the table. "We have an announcement," Mother said.

Father looked at her for a long moment. It was as if some private communication was occurring. He put his knife and fork down and put his hands on the table. He smiled to himself.

We looked at him expectantly.

"What?" I asked. I couldn't read the look in my father's eyes.

At last he spoke. "We're moving."

We erupted in questions. "Where? When? What's the name of the town? Do they play football there? How come?"

"Florida," Dad said. "Fort Lauderdale. As soon as the school year is done. The name of the town is Coral Springs. The name of the high school is Coconut Creek, and yes, they play football. Pretty good football too, from what I've seen on my business trips. I'll be working for a new company in Miami."

"Awww," we cried together at the mention of the hometown of our Super Bowl foes.

"Miami stinks," Timmy said. "They got the Dolphins there!"

"That's alright," Father said. "I realize how much you boys love Texas. We all love Texas. I hope you won't be upset. You shouldn't be. I think you'll like the place. Give it a chance. It's summer there all year-round."

"Where's your ammi?" Bobby piped in.

"It's Miami," Mother said.

"That's what I said," he replied quizzically. "Where's your ammi?"

We all burst out laughing. "It's not 'my ammi,' son," Dad said. "Not like 'yours' or 'mine.' It's a place called Miami."

Bobby remained happily confused. The rest of us jumped in with more questions.

"When are we moving?" I asked.

"As soon as school is out, like I said," Dad replied, smiling at me. "We want to get down there as soon as possible to get settled. I have an apartment we'll be staying at until our house is done being built in August. The apartment building has a pool!"

That revelation caused more excitement. The questions continued, and our excitement lasted well into the evening. In our bedroom that night, we talked about this new place none of us had ever seen.

"Are ya gonna miss Texas?" Willie asked me. I didn't answer right away. Tides were moving back and forth inside me. The first thought I had about leaving Texas was for the land. I loved the land, and it loved me, the same way I knew my mom loved me. The thought of leaving this place on the edge of the Great Plains saddened me.

The other part of me rejoiced. It was the part of me that was growing in ways that would eventually take me away from the woods and pastures I loved as a boy. I was growing toward adulthood and becoming more concerned with man-made things and social constructs. The move would take me away to a place where no one knew me. No one would have cause to call me names that seared my heart.

I shrugged in the dark as I lay in my bed. "Nah," I said finally.

I said nothing to anyone at school about moving. One day, midway through spring training my coach called me into his office after practice.

"Hear y'all are movin', son," he drawled.

In a flash, I saw the writing on the wall. There would be no use for me on the team if I was moving. I'd be asked to quit. I never quit anything in my life.

"No, sir," I replied impulsively, hoping I sounded convincing.

Coach frowned. "Huh?" he said. "I thought yer brother-in-law said you was movin' after the school year."

I shrugged. "Not that I know of, sir."

Coach looked puzzled. "'Kay, son. That's all."

Two days later, I was back in the coach's office trying to explain myself.

"Coach, sorry I lied," I pleaded. "I just don't wanna hafta give up playin'. That's all, sir."

The coach's expression told me he'd already made his decision four decisions ago and had moved on to the next priority.

"Uh-huh," he said absently as he sat at his desk punching holes in papers filled with play diagrams. He didn't bother to look up at me. "It's alright, son. You just go ahead an' clear out yer locker. Good luck to ya."

And so ended my Texas football career. Like it had begun, easily overlooked.

I floated, disconnected through the last couple of weeks of the school year. The few kids that did learn of the move thought it very exciting.

"Man, I hear the girls wear bikinis all the time!" one of my friends who'd never even had a date exclaimed. His eyes were wide behind thick glasses. "Man, I'd go nuts on them down there."

Quickly, it seemed to me, the school year ended. For the next week the house was in bedlam as Mother and Father tried to get the household organized for packing and moving. We boys weren't much help.

Colleen and Eileen, by now out of the house and married, came by often but weren't in much position to help. Colleen was a mother herself now, and Eileen, once so tyrannical and threatening as the boy's summertime babysitter, was herself expecting and looked every bit the glowing mother in waiting.

Somehow, Mother and Father muddled through with a lot of impatient yelling and a few stiff martinis at cocktail time. Finally, the day came in the first week of June when the movers had left in their big tractor-trailer rig with all the furniture and the station wagon was loaded to the gills. We'd be leaving the next morning. Mother told us we were going to make a family vacation out of the move, with stops in New Orleans, Jackson, Mississippi, and Mobile Bay to see the USS *Alabama*. As usual, we would be staying at a Holiday Inn like we always did when we traveled because they all had pools. Everyone was happy.

Everyone except me. I couldn't reconcile my contradictory feelings about moving away. I was grateful to be escaping my torment for the last four years at the hands of Stevie Walsh and the rest of the neighborhood boys. I often dreamed about that night in the tent and when I did I wept in my sleep. I dreaded thinking about my upcoming junior year. My stomach would tie up in knots just thinking about the prospect of sharing a class with Joey and Paul. I was certain they were now openly talking about me with various classmates. I truly felt relieved to be leaving. It felt to me more like a great escape at the last possible moment.

But every time I ventured off the grass of my backyard and into the fields and woods since the move was announced my heart would ache. I spent hours alone at the Swiss Family Robinson tree. Nothing could match this place. I sensed something truly special was passing. I would never go venturing into woods and fields like these again. There was too much asphalt and concrete in Fort Lauderdale. It would be different.

Moving day arrived. The morning dawned grey and threatening. My younger brothers were too keyed up to eat any breakfast. Mother kept going through the home, checking for items left behind or things she would just as soon leave. The noise from the boys was getting under her skin.

"Why don't you boys just go wait in the car!" she growled through gritted teeth. Timmy, Willie, and Bobby dashed out to claim their seats. I followed them out through the utility room, but on a sudden impulse, hooked a right and went out the back door as my brothers continued into the garage. I was alone. My heart was aching to express itself, and I didn't want to be around anyone.

I followed my feet and kept walking. Distant thunder made me look at the sky. Dark grey clouds scudded by low overhead. The rising wind blew my rather long hair back. I leaned my head back. It felt good.

I stepped through the barbed wire fence and into the pasture. I walked up a gentle rise and stood there, looking back over the tank and the dam. I could see the tips of rooftops of the neighborhood falling away out of sight. It began to rain. I looked at the ground under my feet. I could feel the earth's longing for me rising up. I watched as raindrops fell upon the water in the tank, turning its surface into an abstract, shimmering skin. The smell of the clay earth as it became wet rose familiar to my nose. I looked over toward the forest line that marked the beginning of the woods I knew like my own body. Tree branches swayed in the wind.

No grasshoppers rose before me. They were sheltering in the long grass till the storm passed. It began raining harder. I had only a wind-breaker over my tee shirt and shorts. It was soon plastered to my skin. The wind bent the leaves in prayer, as if begging me not to go.

The sky wept. I was leaving. The tears fell in earnest, soaking my head and running down over me and dripping heavily off my shorts, trying to pull me into the ground. The earth wanted to hold me. I felt her tugging, and my heart broke. Tears sprang in my eyes, melded with the rain and ran to the ground, hallowing the spot.

"I'm leaving," I said, choking on the words.

"No!" the wind cried back with the only voice the earth had. She cried harder, beseeching me. The rain felt like a weight on my head and shoulders.

I wept. My tears flowed unabashedly. "I have to go."

"No! Please, no!" I could hear her voice crying in the wind and rain.

"I'm sorry."

"Please!"

I turned and headed for my family. They would be in the car, waiting.

The earth wailed in rain-splattering grief, imploring me to come back. I swore I could hear her calling me through the roar of the downpour. "Danny boy!"

But I was gone.

EPILOGUE

August 1999

"...I'll simply sleep in peace until you come to me...
And kneel and say an 'Ave' there for me..."

As I headed north toward Lake Texoma along Farm Road 1417, away from town and my old neighborhood, the land began to resemble the landscape of my youth. There was the occasional new residential development and a new overpass, otherwise, the land looked as I remembered it. I passed the old Air Force base that had become a community college, regional airport and business park. I was surprised how familiar the land felt, even after a lifetime away. The sky still came right down to the ground, the cattle in the fields were the familiar brown and white, and the tanks still looked muddy and green. I drove along the rolling land, my mind reliving the past.

It had been almost thirty years since I had left my youth in Texas. The family move to Fort Lauderdale was a soul-saving reprieve for me. My arrival in South Florida was cleansing. As I made new friends and became acquainted with a new high school I felt reborn.

Everything represented a new beginning. As a new prospect with my high school football team, having come from Texas high school football and the reputation that carried provided an opportunity to finally shine. I made the most of it. Despite a knee injury that ended my junior season early, I came back for my senior year even more determined and more in shape. That season I led the entire county in receptions and led my team in touchdowns scored. I was named to the all-county team and a national high school All-American as a wide receiver.

Making friends and dating girls seem to come naturally for me. I loved the tropical climate and going to the beach all year long. My senior year of high school was a dream come true. I no longer felt like a haunted little boy.

I grew my hair long and sported long sideburns. I argued with my Republican-leaning parents about Vietnam, Nixon, and Watergate. I installed an 8-track stereo and shag carpeting in the family's second car, a '67 Mustang. My gang of friends, mostly football teammates, some of the cheerleaders, and other various hangers-on, would meet in the evenings at the McDonald's in Margate, crowd ourselves into a couple of cars, and head for the beach. I had a steady girlfriend. My heart was light, I was quick and fleet of foot, and my soul felt free.

In many ways, and for a long, long time, that senior year of high school was the zenith of my life. After graduation, I had returned to Texas to play football for a small college south of Fort Worth. I left with high hopes and dreams of continuing my football career. It was, however, the point where I set my life adrift for the next ten years.

In less than a week of college football I lost my passion and motivation for the game. I didn't know why exactly. The game suddenly meant little to me. Perhaps it was because I found myself struggling again, a fast but still small athlete who was playing alongside much-bigger players. I was taking a pounding. Perhaps it was because I was away from home for the first time, and although I wasn't homesick, I felt untethered.

Maybe it was because I met Patty. She was a vivacious, flirtatious young siren who brought me the gift of sexual awakening. She was a great teacher, and I was a very willing learner. Together, we lit the fires of desire in each other that became all-consuming. I didn't last my first semester in the classroom. She was all that mattered.

After my ouster from school at the end of the semester, I found a job and an apartment close to campus where Patty and I continued our odyssey, entwined and enmeshed day and night until one fateful night in early February when I answered an angry, late-night pounding on my door to find Patty's six-foot-four father standing there in a ten-gallon hat and a gun in his hand. He strode in past me without a word to the bedroom where his daughter lay in my bed.

"Get dressed," he growled.

She hurriedly pulled on some clothes and beat a hasty retreat out the door where her mother stood waiting in the yard, barely glancing my way.

Her father walked over to the door and looked down at her. "We paid for you to live in your dorm room like a White woman. Not over here like a whore."

Then he turned and looked down at me. He towered over me. "If I ever see you again," he said low and menacing, poking a finger into my chest, "I'll kill ya."

I looked into the man's eyes and believed him. I believed every word. Patty's father turned and walked out. "Get in the truck," he said to them both.

The pickup backed into the street as I came out into the yard. I watched as they drove away. Patty gave a quick glance back in my direction. It was the last time I ever saw her.

I was too ashamed to go home to my parents, who had moved the family from Fort Lauderdale to New Hampshire when I had left for college. I ignored their pleading and cajoling to come home. Instead, I sold whatever few possessions I had, mailed some personal things to my parents I wanted to keep, left a month's rent in cash along with a letter for my landlord in an envelope, and left. I didn't bother to show up at work to quit my low-wage factory job. I walked through town with a canvas duffel bag filled with a few changes of clothes slung over my shoulder and a pawn shop guitar in my hand out to Highway 67 and stuck my thumb out. I had eighteen dollars in my pocket.

I spent the next four months on the road hitchhiking throughout the Southwest, living hand to mouth, working a day or two here and there washing dishes or hauling hay. I spent my time in honky-tonk bars, truck stops, and sleeping on the couches of strangers. I got drunk with sinners and cooked up quick money making schemes with people I thought were saints. Increasingly, I found myself subverting my integrity for a full stomach, a few cold beers and a joint, a few extra bucks and the occasional romp with any woman willing to play along with me. I wasn't above petty criminal activity to get by on.

Hitchhiking down Highway 54 from the Guadalupe Mountains toward Van Horn, Texas in early May, I fell in with three other drifters, luckless losers looking for their next big score. For the next week or so I helped them run bales of marijuana coming up from Mexico to a remote landing strip out on Farm Road 2185 and running it into Van Horn. There, we passed it off to a couple of dangerous-looking older men who looked like they'd seen their share of time behind bars. Sitting alone in a bar late one night along Interstate 10 outside of town after passing off a load of weed, exchanging the money and taking my cut, I stared drunkenly into my beer and wondered where I was going to sleep. It occurred to me that Van Horn was a town I'd ticked off on my escape route to Cuidad Juarez from my family all those years ago, before my boyhood was ruined. I felt an old anger brewing deep down inside me.

Highways like Interstate 10, with its long stretches of Southwestern isolation, began to wear on me. By the end of May, I'd had enough of living like a nomad, rootless and disconnected. I called my parents collect from a rundown truck stop in the middle of nowhere New Mexico and told them I was ready to come home.

Relieved beyond words to hear from me, they wired money for a one-way plane ticket from Dallas to Boston. In two days, I made my way across west Texas to Dallas/Fort Worth International. On the plane I sat in my seat sunburnt and tired, thinking about the desert heat, the most spectacular night skies I'd ever seen sleeping under the stars, a girl whose name I couldn't remember, and the sex we enjoyed at a ranch I worked at for a week outside of Abilene, the friendly-trucker who taught me a few Dylan tunes on my beat up old guitar, and the truck stop chicken fried steak and gravy I devoured anytime I had a couple of bucks. I was glad to be headed for New Hampshire.

———◆———

I stayed home a little over a year, working for a small furniture-making operation in Ossipee, enjoying the smell of sawdust and working with my hands. Just being in New Hampshire felt good. It felt like a place I belonged to. Still, I wasn't very goal-oriented or self-directed. A shadow lay deep inside me. I sort of floated along, not thinking too much about my future.

I tried college again, briefly. Again, I was asked not to come back after a year. A friend of mine from the school invited me back to his hometown in southern Maine, near Kittery. There, I met and fell in love with a sweet, simple farm girl. Realizing it was probably time to make some decisions and set some goals in my life, I asked the farm girl to marry me, then went down to the recruiting station in Portsmouth and enlisted in the Air Force.

I had a sense of pride serving my country and enjoyed having a job where I carried an M-16 gun as my daily tool for my assigned duties. But I had a sophomoric stubbornness when it came to basic military tenets of authority and conformity. After living a rootless and irresponsible life for the past few years, I found myself chafing under the discipline demanded by the military. The malaise America experienced after Vietnam left its military seemingly schizophrenic, with much of its personnel hardened Vietnam vets who remained in a culture they could understand, and an influx during the late '70s of young recruits who'd grown up questioning everything, especially the Vietnam experience. I was typical of many who joined after Vietnam. Most seemed to be joining out of simple, personal reasons such as the desire for a steady job, escape from dead-end towns and lives, or simply because they were without any other prospects. I just felt like I needed to do something, anything, to move forward.

I did see some of the world, however. After basic training and tech school in San Antonio, I came home and married the farm girl. Together, we spent the next two years stationed at a small base in the middle of England, living in a small village off base and spending our time in the local pub. I fell in with a fellow airman, Allan, who in his civilian life was a hippie from the Berkshire Mountains of Massachusetts. We had done our combat training together and discovered we were both assigned to the same overseas base. We became fast friends. For the first time since my heyday with Billy Swift, I had a best friend again.

What we enjoyed most together, along with our wives, was an easygoing, hippie lifestyle. We concluded that the best reason we could come up with for joining the military in the first place was so that we would meet. That logic suited us both. We became like brothers and spent the next two years in England doing what hippies like to do; we smoked a lot of hashish and spent time off at home getting high, making love to our wives, writing songs, and playing guitar. We barely tolerated working on the flight line at the air base. We were about as irresponsible as anyone carrying a deadly weapon could be without getting caught. We took advantage of our positions controlling access to restricted areas and being on remote patrols together. We would crouch in hidden areas of the base late at night, smoking hash out of a crude pipe made from a soda can with holes poked in the sides with the stickpin of our military police badges.

My wife and I had a child while we were stationed in England. I brought her to the hospital in Banbury on an early morning in late July, under a typically grey English sky. When I left the hospital that afternoon, high from that feeling of instant, unconditional love I felt upon seeing our daughter born, I was surprised by a spectacular blue sky, bright sun, and wispy white clouds that greeted me overhead. From that day onward I called my daughter Sunshine. The nickname stuck. I suddenly felt as if I had something more to live for.

The lifestyle I was leading, however, being married and having a daughter notwithstanding, still hadn't progressed beyond my own limited outlook on life or desire for nothing more than one good time leading to another. My cavalier behavior put me on a collision course with military expectations. I should have known better.

Back stateside and with less than six months left in my enlistment, both Allan and I faced court-martial, charged with smoking marijuana and using cocaine on duty. It was the height of Ronald Reagan's 'morning in America' and the conservative bend of the times landed on us with both feet. While awaiting trial one day, I summoned every bit of courage I could muster and went to explain my predicament to my father. I sat in the car in my parents' driveway for a long while before trudging up the front steps. My good father, an ex-Marine and decorated veteran of World War II, was waiting apprehensively inside. He wasn't sure what to expect from my visit.

I stammered out my sad tale, barely able to look my father in the eye. I died a thousand deaths as my father stood listening with a dark scowl on his face. Finally, my voice trailed off, and I stopped. My father stared coldly at me for a moment, saying nothing. Finally, he spoke.

"You don't know how deeply you've disappointed your mother and me," he said. He turned and walked away, leaving me standing in place, looking down at the floor. Never had I felt so low as I did right then.

My farm girl wife sat at the back of the courtroom eight months pregnant. She watched with a worried expression as her husband was sentenced to five months at hard labor, then escorted by the SPs out of court and over to the base jail. They were long months for both of us. I was released just before Thanksgiving and came home to my wife, daughter, and a son who was born while I was doing my time. I had no job, no place of my own, and no ambition other than to mellow out next to my record collection and smoke a joint.

⇒

For the next several years I walked around with a chip on my shoulder and a shadow in my soul. I was angry at the world and ready to blame anyone but myself for the consequences of my behavior. Allan had drifted back to the Berkshires. Meanwhile, I, who by virtue of a curious mind, a native intelligence, and articulate vocabulary, possessed of a potential if I would only choose to engage myself, settled instead for drifting from dead-end job to dead-end job. Angry, dissatisfied with myself and my place in life, I drowned my unhappiness drinking, partying, smoking pot, and snorting cocaine.

These were my lost years. From aborted attempts at college to hitchhiking lonely highways, irresponsible behavior in the military to incarceration, and from dead-end job to dead-end job, I drifted without direction. I quickly learned to lie about my incarceration after having a few doors slammed in my face. At times, my marriage became strained. My only grounding joy was my children. I remained in my fog, living with a deep-seated anger that occasionally roiled my stomach whenever painful memories or frustrations about the state of my life came to mind. I wanted to believe I was worth more than I had to show for myself. I wanted to do something meaningful. I had no idea how to make that desire real.

⬥

It was a lucky break, really. Just before an Emergency Medical Technician certification I obtained during my military days expired, I landed a job with a small private ambulance company. Something clicked inside me. For the first time, I was actually helping others. I was helping others during the worst moments of their lives. The realization ricocheted in my mind till it found a place to land… right in that lonely, frightened, and painful place where a boyhood trauma had lain for years as an unhealed wound. In that instant, I had a purpose. In that instant, I realized that what had happened all those years ago in a tent at Boy Scout camp wasn't my fault. Not my fault at all. Much like the victims of injury and disease I was tending to in the back of an ambulance. Usually through no fault of their own, my patients were having the worst day of their lives and I was there to help make a difference. I began to hold my head up.

That lucky break led to an even bigger one. Most of my coworkers were volunteer firefighters. I would listen all day long while they regaled each other with tales of fighting fires. I suspected sometimes that these tales had the quality of a good fishing story because they seemed to grow over time. But they were very entertaining.

I walked into the station kitchen one morning to excited talk about a nearby city that was conducting an entrance exam for full-time firefighter positions.

"Hey," one of my coworkers called over to me, "the four of us are going over to take the test. You oughtta take it with us!"

I smiled and shrugged. My grandfather and uncle had been career firefighters in New Jersey. I'd visited their fire station many times when I was a kid. For some reason, I never gave becoming one much thought. But I listened to the enthusiasm of my coworkers and about the better pay and benefits.

"Maybe I will," I said.

I was the only one from work, including the vollies who had urged me to apply, who showed up on a Saturday morning for the written and physical exam. I passed with flying colors. I completed the entrance process and one evening in late October, two weeks shy of my twenty-ninth birthday, I walked into the fire station lugging my gear and reported for duty to the shift captain. I had never put out anything bigger than a campfire in my life. I had burned several acres of dry brush as a kid once and burned down an empty garage as a teenager, but thought that probably wasn't worth mentioning during my interview. I instantly felt I had found my calling. The bond of brotherhood that is the hallmark of the fire service answered a deep-seated desire for connection, forging a close-knit family with my coworkers, sharing something few others ever get to experience. I was sharing bonds of love and camaraderie while experiencing the extremes of New England firefighting, saving lives and protecting property. I became the third generation from my family to become a firefighter.

I had a second son. Three children completed me. My father was proud of me, which meant more than I could express. I became the recipient of various keepsakes from my grandfather and uncle's fire careers, retrieved from the attic by my father. On the mantle of my home I kept my grandfather's one hundred-year-old Cairns & Brother's leather fire helmet. Keeping the tradition alive, I also wore a Cairns & Brother's leather helmet.

That was more than twenty-five years ago. I had learned plenty about myself in that time. I learned what fulfillment felt like. I witnessed how fragile life was. I learned the meaning of courage.

But the sometimes harsh lessons in life didn't stop there. An old shadow lay across my soul. Though grounded now in a fulfilling profession, a wild heart and a tendency for impulsiveness sometimes made my life wobbly. My passion for the fire service took me away from home for days at a time. I would occasionally disappear on carousing benders with friends or fellow firefighters. Sometimes the only thing I took seriously was firefighting.

The toll finally extracted its price on my marriage, and on a grey day in April, my sweet, farm girl wife left and moved into her own apartment. Eventually the divorce settlement had me with custody of my two sons while Sunshine, now twelve years old, moved in with her mother. The unintended consequences, losing the only house I'd ever bought, separated children, recriminations from my growing, questioning children, and the next fourteen years of living without a companion seared my soul with hard wisdom.

I stood and paid the price. I learned to accept the consequences of my behavior and made myself grow. I entered counseling. I went back to college at night and earned a degree. I learned to thrive on lean and lonely living. I struggled to be an effective parent. In time, I learned to carry the weight of my regrets and failures as a part of who I was, rather than as a ball and chain. I learned forgiveness.

And then, luck struck again. In a dark and lonely moment, I asked God to send me someone to love. Someone who would love me even though I didn't always deserve it. It didn't matter so much to me what she looked like. As long as I could see her beauty, as long as we could deeply connect and we could make each other laugh, I would be happy. A year later, she found me. It made all the difference. Her presence in my life made me want to be a better man, and after a few years carefully blending both of her adult children with my own now grown children into a large extended family, those five children were our wedding party. Allan, who over the years would come and go free-spiritedly in and out of my life, officiated.

"...And I shall sleep in peace until you come to me..."

Lost in thought, I almost missed the turn that would take me the last mile to Camp Grayson. Pulling myself back to the present, I started looking for the camp entrance that memory told me was somewhere up on the left. Finally, I spotted it. I pulled the rental car off the faded blacktop road into the dirt entrance. I looked up at the arched gateway. Camp Grayson had been renamed. The sign over the gate listed someone's name. I wondered if that person was now dead and if he'd been a past camper. I know a lot about death. I've seen it many times over the years in my work.

I drove through the gateway, pulled over, and shut down the car and got out. The late-afternoon sun blazed down on me. I reminded myself that at least it was a dry heat, not the hazy, hot, and humid summers I'd become accustomed to in New Hampshire. It didn't have much effect. It was damn hot, I thought.

I walked up the dirt road a little ways, remembering the cedar pines and oak trees that still wooded the area.

"Can I help you, sir?"

I looked around to see a man in a khaki shirt under a stand of cedar trees raking pine needles. I guessed him to be in his early twenties.

I walked toward the young man. "Hi, there," I said smiling.

"Howdy. What can I do for ya?"

"Camped here as a kid," I explained, squinting in the sun. "Back in the sixties before I moved away."

Curious, the young man approached. "Name's Jack Viers," he said in a friendly tone. He extended a hand.

"Danny," I replied.

We shook hands. "I'm the camp ranger," Jack said. "So, you camped here as a kid, huh? The sixties?"

"Yeah," I replied, looking around.

"Man, that was a long time ago."

I gave a sideways glance toward the young ranger. I smiled. I could feel the sun creasing the lines of my face. "Yeah, it was."

"Things ain't changed all that much," Jack said. "Some new buildings over the years and stuff. Had an electrical fire a few years back that burned one of the old buildings. We rebuilt though. We're an all-year-round camp now."

"That so?" I said.

"Yes, sir. We do alright."

"Glad to hear it. I was, uh, wondering. I'm just here visiting the area. Would you mind if I just looked around a little? For old-time's sake?"

Jack lifted his baseball cap and scratched a sweaty hairline. "Don't see why not, I s'pose. Next group of campers ain't due till tomorrow. Go ahead, have a look around."

"Appreciate it," I said.

"Gotta go finish my rakin'," Jack said. "Nice to meet ya."

"Likewise."

We shook hands again.

I watched Jack walk away, rake in hand. I turned and looked up the rutted road to where it bent right and disappeared behind some trees. A cloud passed through my mind as I stood with my hands in my pockets. I thought, this is where we gathered for the welcome speech each year. I started humming softly to myself. My lips moved slightly. Words to the tune came, whispered softly into the dry air.

"G-R-A-Y-S-O-N spells Grayson, Grayson. That's the place where all the scouts go, scouts go. The man who runs it is a hobo, hobo...."

I began walking up the road, following it around the bend. I tried hard to remember details about the land, but so far nothing seemed familiar. If anything, the land seemed a bit more closed in. I thought, it has to be that little kid perspective kind of thing, where everything seems big. Till you see it again as an adult. Kind of like walking into your first-grade class when you're all grown up and looking at all those tiny seats. I smiled to myself.

I followed the road to an opening surrounded by large pines and oak trees. Remnants of an old building lay tiredly on the ground, baking in the sun. It was the old chow hall, I thought. I turned to look through the trees. If I was right, then my old Scout troop camping area was somewhere over in that direction. I could see a small meadow beyond, beckoning me.

I walked through the woods toward the field. Emerging from the trees I stopped, studying the terrain. It felt right. I remembered my troop's usual campground assignment wasn't far from the main entrance and the old chow hall. I gazed over the field.

I had that old feeling in the pit of my stomach. The feeling I always got being on the land. I could feel the ground underneath, welcoming me. I felt connected to the earth. I felt like I belonged.

I began walking slowly across the meadow. It was perhaps an acre in size, ringed by cedar, oak, and mesquite trees. I looked back and forth, scanning the ground. Occasionally I would see a ring of rocks that marked a campfire. This is where we planted our Choctaw flag, I thought as I looked down at the ground in the center of the field. I smiled once again, remembering the homemade flag with its profile of an Indian chief.

I looked over toward one corner of the field. Over there, I thought. Over there. I felt a pulling in my heart. I walked slowly and deliberately toward the woods at the edge of the field. I came to where the trees began and hesitated. I peered into the woods. The ground sloped gently down and away, rose, and then fell away again. I felt sure I was in the right place.

I walked into the woods a little ways. Evidence of previous tent sites were scattered around through the trees. I turned and looked back out toward the field. This is right, I thought. Our tents would be here where we could see the field and keep watch over our flag. I was here. So was a small boy, looking out from the hidden places of my heart.

I looked around at the graveyard of my boyhood. The earth beneath me offered her mute testimony. This was where a boyhood died and a new person, wounded, uncertain of myself and alone, had emerged, not knowing my way or what I should do. I was lost for a long time. My vision blurred with sudden tears.

I do not know how long I stood there weeping for the small boy who laughed and played in the palm of God till one day, when God turned away for just a moment, I was snared by a cruelty in the guise of a bigger, stronger, and angry teenage boy.

The tears surprised me. Long ago I thought I had reconciled what had happened here and come to terms. A simple realization that what happened was not my fault. I was not to blame, much as the other boys in the neighborhood had blared it to my face. The realization had enabled me to remember all the other wonderful things about my boyhood that the tragic episode in the tent that night had overshadowed in my mind for many years. And yet, I wondered if I had truly reconciled that night in Stevie's tent and if I was still bearing the consequences.

I thought about the others. I wondered if Stevie Walsh was a good person now or a monster. I wondered about Billy Swift, the only best friend I ever had as a boy. I had never seen or heard from him again after I moved away. I thought of the Black kids I'd gone to school with in junior high. I wondered if they believed their lives were any better now in their town.

My life since then has traveled many paths, both high and low. Looking at the hallowed ground around me I asked myself, am I a good man? Am I a man that hurt little boy would be glad he became?

A strong feeling swept over me as I stood in the quiet of the shady ground. The smell of cedar floated by in the warm breeze. In my mind the ghost of a boy with his skinny frame, mop of brown hair and aching heart that I carried inside me for so long, began to smile. I smiled back. Sunlight waved gently through the trees. Peace settled on my soul. I slipped out of my shoes and socks and stood barefoot on the soft ground. The earth remembered me.

"Oh, Danny boy, oh, Danny boy, I love you so."

The End

CREDITS &
ACKNOWLEDGEMENTS

Some of the passages regarding the murder & lynching of George Hughes were cited from the following source:

Nolan Thompson, SHERMAN RACE RIOT OF 1930 Handbook of Texas Online
http://www.tshaonline.org/handbook/online/articles/jes06
accessed November 16, 2011 Published by the Texas State Historical Association

Grateful thanks to the following for their love, advice, critique and encouragement:

Kristin; my first editor, Abbi Lundborn, Ginna Schonwald, Fernando Valdivia, Kathie Routhier and the rest of The Pondview Readers, Sue Wheeler & Dover Adult Education, Water Street Bookstore, Douglas Richard, Melanie Fair, Cortney Farmer, Megan McIntyre, the town of Bridgeton, Maine, my brothers & sisters; we're still loud, boisterous and warm, and our parents who kept it all together for us. A special thanks to Jackson McIntyre.

CPSIA information can be obtained at www.ICGtesting.com
Printed in the USA
LVOW121349011012

300969LV00001B/38/P